TINY
TRADITIONS

By Sylvia Trygg Voudrie

Sylvia Voudrie

CHITRA PUBLICATIONS

Chitra Publications
2 Public Avenue
Montrose, Pennsylvania 18801

First printing: 1992

Library of Congress Cataloging-in-Publication Data.

Voudrie, Sylvia Trygg, 1938-
    Tiny Traditions / by Sylvia Trygg Voudrie
        p.   cm.
    Includes bibliographical references.
    ISBN 0-9622565-2-8 : $9.95
    1. Patchwork--Patterns. 2. Miniature quilts. I. Title.
TT835.V68 1992
746.9'7'0228--dc20   92-16803
                                                           CIP

Editor: Patti Lilik Bachelder
Design and Illustrations: Mark D. Wayman
Photographs: Stephen J. Appel Photography, Vestal, New York

PREFACE

I bought my first book on the subject of miniature quilt making in 1987. The quilts were beautiful, but the methods looked too complicated. To ensure precision, you had to draw different grids on paper, tape them to a flat surface, draw the lines from the grid onto your fabric and finally cut the strips and squares. That was not for me! I did not even attempt to make one of those quilts.

Several years later I purchased another book on miniatures. This quilter used a similar system, but this time I decided to make one of these little treasures, believing that I could be just as accurate in cutting the pieces without drawing the grids. I cut the strips and pieces using rulers and a rotary cutter, just as I had been doing for larger quilts—and it worked!

And it will work for you, too. Use the suggestions and patterns in this book to develop your skills in making miniature quilts, and then EXPERIMENT! There is more than one way to make a miniature quilt. Try different techniques. Find out which methods work best *for you*. I hope you will combine a smattering of techniques from several quilters to develop some of your very own techniques. Only you are uniquely you!

DEDICATION

"Now unto him who is able to do exceedingly abundantly above all that we ask or think..." Ephesians 4:20

WHY NOT MINIATURES?

Why would you want to make miniature quilts? Why not make quilts for a more practical purpose? Quilters and non-quilters alike have asked similar questions. Here are a dozen good reasons:

1. You can make miniature quilts at minimal cost.
2. You can use your fabric stash and keep it too. We can't say that about cake!
3. You can make a large collection of small quilts, from all the patterns you love. "So many quilts, so little time!"
4. You can expand your quilting skills. It takes precision techniques to make miniatures.
5. You can hand quilt miniatures anywhere. They are small and portable.
6. You can avoid the boredom of doing the same thing, over and over.
7. You can make a whole quilt in a short time.
8. You can enjoy the satisfaction of completing your quilting projects. We can't always say that about larger quilts.
9. You can hang them, stack them in an open cupboard or use them as accessories with dolls and bears. Storage space is not a problem.
10. You can try a new pattern in a small size before making it in a larger size.
11. You can give great gifts to your friends and family.
12. You can experiment with your own original ideas. If an idea fails, it is not a great loss of money or time—try another.

But let me warn you before you get started! Miniature quilt making is addictive! You will know that you are addicted when those around you notice a glazed, abstract expression on your face while they talk. You do not hear them, because your mind has slipped into "miniature quilt land." It has truly become a strong addiction when you find yourself unable to sleep at night because your mind is filled with new designs and techniques you'd like to try next. Maybe you will even get out of bed in the middle of the night to sew!

Making miniature quilts has been a rewarding experience in my life. If you already love to quilt, why not miniatures? If you are just learning to quilt, why not miniatures? Why not get started now!

TABLE OF CONTENTS

EQUIPMENT

Rotary cutter

I prefer the large size rotary cutter. Do not tighten the screw on the cutter too tightly or you will have difficulty cutting fabric. The screw should be just tight enough for the blade to turn firmly but easily. Always keep a spare blade on hand to replace a dull one.

Cutting mats

The most versatile size is probably 18" x 24". Even for miniature quilts, you still need a mat large enough to make long strip cuts. I also have a very small one that is great for the last step in joining the binding on a quilt.

Rulers

Accurate rulers are essential for the precision cuts that result in perfectly made miniature quilts. My favorite sizes are:

6" x 12" for most strip cuts

3" x 18" for long first cuts and long bias cuts

4" square: This little gem has 1/16" markings, which are needed for many of these quilts.

6" square with a 45° angle marked corner-to-corner for cutting bias squares. The lines on my 6" square are easier to read than those on the 4" square, so I tend to use this one most often. It's one of my favorite tools!

Sandpaper

This is my other favorite tool. You just can't beat using a fine-grained sandpaper with adhesive backing on the bottom of all your rulers to keep them from slipping during use. (See "Basic Cutting Instructions.")

Drafting tape

It's great for "marking" your rulers in order to make special cuts, and for making a seam guide on your sewing machine. It leaves no residue.

Sewing Machine

You do not need a fancy machine, but it must be in good condition to produce good work. Be sure that the tension is correctly adjusted and that your machine sews a good seam. If not, have it serviced.

Sewing machine needles

A "small" needle will prevent distortion of small pieces; size 70 or 80 (9 or 11) will not leave holes in the fabric.

Thread

I once heard a quilter say, "Thread is thread." Not so! Buy good quality thread. It won't get fuzzy or unwind during sewing, and it won't break unless you want it to. Save money by using cones of thread and a cone holder.

Seam ripper

This is not only for taking out bad seams and mistakes. It also makes a great tool for guiding the fabric pieces under the sewing machine's presser foot.

Thread clippers

Using thread clippers to snip chain-pieced units apart is much quicker than using scissors.

Long, fine straight pins

The pins that are labeled "quilter's pins" are long, but they are too heavy for tiny pieces. Look for fine pins, preferably the ones with glass heads.

Magnetized pin holder

This is not necessary, but it is absolutely terrific! You can practically throw pins at it.

Ironing surface and steam iron

Some quilters do not use steam, but I find it essential for setting seams and straightening any distortions. Keep the iron on the lowest heat setting for steam; you do not want to give your cotton fabrics a "shiner."

Spot remover

Keep a good spot remover on hand, one that does not leave any residue on fabric. You never know when a spot might appear on one of your tiny treasures!

SELECTING FABRICS

Choose only light to medium weight, closely woven 100 percent cotton fabrics. Blends do not look or feel as good, or take stitching as well as cottons. Batting also tends to "beard" through blends; the fibers migrate to the surface of the quilt, making it fuzzy. Since you will be using very little fabric in each miniature quilt, why not use the best quality fabric available?

Usually, small to medium print fabrics are the best choices. A medium print looks large on a tiny quilt. However, I am not dogmatic about the size of prints. There are too many variables. It is helpful to draw 1/2" shapes on a 3" x 5" card and cut them out to reveal windows. Hold this card over potential fabrics to judge how each will look when cut into miniature pieces.

It is essential that there be good contrast between two fabrics that are next to each other. Otherwise, they will blend together. For this reason, monochromatic color schemes do not seem to work very well in tiny quilts. An often used plan is to choose a multi-colored fabric that you love and select other fabrics to match the colors in that print.

Vary the intensity of the colors, using light, medium and dark values of each, and vary the types of prints. It is boring if everything looks the same. Use solids, small plaids, narrow stripes, random prints, prints that appear to be solids from a distance, and florals. Lay potential fabrics together, stand back, and squint. Try to visualize them together in your quilt. Maybe one print is too large for miniature pieces but would make a great border. Wallpaper-type/striped prints make terrific borders with mitered corners.

Study other quilts and pictures of quilts. Do not be afraid to ask for advice, but trust your own instinct. You don't need an art course to know what you like best. Your quilt should reflect your personality, not someone else's.

To Wash or Not To Wash?

Most quilters say wash all your fabric before using it, without exception, or you may be sorry when you later wash the quilt. Certain color dyes may bleed into other fabrics.

My preference is to use unwashed fabric in miniature quilts. It has more body and is easier to handle. These quilts will not be handled roughly so vigorous washing will not be needed.

If you choose not to wash your fabrics, it is a good idea to color test them before use. Cut 2" squares of each fabric and drop them into separate glasses of hot water. Allow them to soak for about fifteen minutes. If color bleeds into the water from any of the fabrics, either do not use it or wash all fabrics in warm water with a mild soap. I prefer Orvus paste for washing fabrics. Rinse thoroughly and tumble in the dryer until almost dry. Spray the cloth with a fabric sizing as you press, to restore body. (Sizing spray is also great for pressing the center crease out of fabric, too.)

In order to hold my rulers securely on the fabric during rotary cutting, I find it essential to place small pieces of adhesive-backed sandpaper on the bottom of all my rulers. You can purchase a whole package of fine-grained sandpaper with adhesive backing very inexpensively. It is made for electric sanders.

Cut the sandpaper into small squares or use a standard size hole puncher to quickly punch out uniform circles. Position them on the bottom of your rulers along the cutting edges, about every two inches. Place a few pieces on each side of the diagonal or bias line of your square ruler to help keep the bias line securely centered on the seam line when you are cutting bias squares.

Cutting Strips

Most of the pieces used to make the quilts in this book are cut from strips, so you must know how to cut perfectly straight narrow strips across the width of the fabric (usually 44"). The lengthwise and crosswise grain on most fabric is not perfectly straight. Usually this does not pose a problem unless it is very obviously distorted. Sometimes there are portions of the distorted fabric where the grain lines are more true. If so, try to cut your strips from these sections. You can always cut individual pieces in the distorted areas. Because these are tiny quilts, you will not need to cut many long strips, except for borders and binding.

My instructions are for right handed quilters. Simply reverse the procedure if you are left handed.

1.   Fold the fabric in half, lining up the selvages. The center fold is sometimes distorted when fabric is wrapped onto the bolt, so do not go by that fold to line up the selvages. You may have to move the selvage of the top layer to the left or right and make a new center fold.

2.   Always start with a perfectly straight-cut left edge. Take your square ruler and line it up with the fold on the bottom, near the left edge of the fabric. With your left hand, place the long ruler against the square ruler. Remove the square ruler with your right hand. Take the rotary cutter and begin cutting just below the bottom fold and continue along the edge of the long ruler, cutting away from yourself. Apply pressure with your left hand to keep the ruler in place. (Those little pieces of sandpaper are also doing their job at keeping the ruler from slipping.) Walk your fingers up the ruler, parallel to the rotary cutter in your right hand, and make the first cut. This is the longest, most difficult cut to make. *Always cut away from your body.*

3.   Now bring the bottom fold up to meet the selvages and line up the (4) cut edges. From now on, you can make shorter cuts through all the layers. Find the line on the ruler for the width of strip needed, align the ruler with the fabric's straight-cut left edge and make your cut. If you are cutting many strips, check the left edge frequently and re-straighten if needed.

Cutting Squares and Rectangles

When a pattern requires a large number of squares and

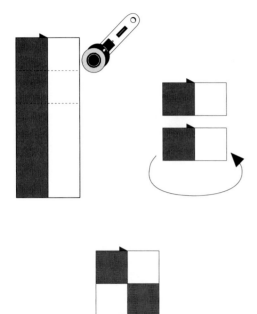

Fig. 1

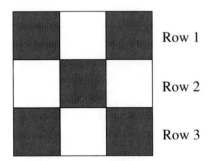

Row 1

Row 2

Row 3

Fig. 2

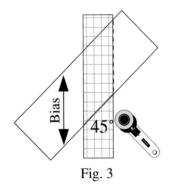

Fig. 3

rectangles, they are subcut from strips. The width of the strip is determined by the finished width of the squares or rectangles required, plus their seam allowance.

FORMULA: Strip width to cut = Finished size of squares or rectangles plus 1/4" for seam allowances.

Use the square ruler to cut same-size squares or rectangles of the required length. If you do not need many pieces, they can be cut individually. Just remember to add the seam allowance to the finished size before cutting.

Cutting Strips That Have Been Sewn Together
Many of the patterns in this book are subcut from strips that have been sewn together first. It is necessary not only to cut precise strips, but also to sew these strips together with precise 1/8" seam allowances. Do not hurry the stitching. Any discrepancy is magnified when stitching miniature quilts. Remember the admonition to keep on the straight and narrow!
Four-Patch and Nine-Patch are two examples of blocks made by first sewing strips together into "set-ups," subcutting them into segments and then arranging and sewing those segments together to form the blocks. For the Four-Patch, sew together two contrasting strips of equal widths. Press the seam allowance toward the darker fabric. Subcut this set-up into two segments which are equal to the finished size of a single square plus its seam allowance.

EXAMPLE: If the finished size of a single square is 1/2", you would need two segments that are each cut 3/4".

Place the two segments right sides together, with contrasting squares opposing each other. The pressed seam allowances will butt each other in opposite directions. Stitch the seam and press, (Fig. 1).
For the Nine-Patch unit, two set-ups are required; one for Rows 1 and 3 and one for Row 2, (Fig. 2). Cut two segments from one set-up and one segment from the other. The technique is the same as that for the Four-Patch unit.

Cutting Half-Square Triangle Units, or Bias Squares
To make these units in miniature sizes, I find the most accurate method is that devised by quilter Nancy J. Martin of That Patchwork Place, Inc. Her technique uses her 6" Bias Square™. Other square rulers will also do the job if they have a center diagonal line and 1/8" markings. If you have the Bias Square™ ruler, be sure that you measure to the outside of the lines and not to the inside. The width of that one line around the square is needed.

1. To make several units of the same two-fabric combinations:
   a. Cut a bias strip of each fabric the same width as the cut size of the bias squares that are required. Cut the two strips about the same length. Use the 45° angle line of the ruler to find the true bias of the fabric, (Fig. 3).

b. Stitch the two strips together on the long bias edge with a 1/8" seam. Press seam toward the dark.

c. Align the diagonal line on the square ruler with the seam line. Near the bottom of the strip, align the ruler for the correct size square. Cut the top two sides of the square unit. Turn this segment around and line up the two sides that were just cut, then cut the third and fourth sides, (Fig. 4).

d. Continue this procedure to cut the required number of bias squares. You do not have to turn each segment around one at a time to cut the third and fourth sides. Just keep cutting the first two sides of all the units you need by allowing enough distance between these first cuts to come back afterwards and cut the third and fourth sides of each bias square unit in succession.

2. To make many units of the same fabric combinations, pairs of bias strip combinations can be stitched together. The cutting procedure is the same as above, but this combining of pairs will eliminate much waste of fabric, (Fig. 5).

3. To make only one or two bias square units, I use this quick method. Cut two contrasting squares of the required cut-size unit. Place right sides together and sew a diagonal seam. Press the darker fabric to its corner. Trim the seam allowance of the two lower pieces to 1/8". Sewing a bias seam on two squares is a snap compared to sewing two tiny triangles together on the bias! It also eliminates cutting bias strips to make just a few units, (Fig. 6).

Connector Squares

Mary Ellen Hopkins defines this technique as using connector corners. These little squares really are quick and accurate. The technique is high on my list of technique "musts"! It is used in several of the patterns in this book. There is very little waste of fabric because we are dealing with small patterns and pieces.

To alternate a Nine-Patch block with a Snowball block, (Fig. 7):
1. Cut a large square the same size as the Nine-Patch block, plus its seam allowance. Then cut four little squares the size of one of the Nine-Patch squares, plus seam allowances, (Fig. 8).
2. Place each little square in a corner of the large square, right sides together, and sew diagonal seams, (Fig. 9).

There are three options for sewing these diagonal seams:
1. Eyeball the seam line.
2. First draw a diagonal guideline.
3. Finger press a diagonal line.
Press each square back to its corner. For our little quilts, trim the two lower layers (the seam allowance) to 1/8".

Fig. 4

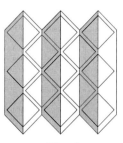

Fig. 5

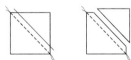

Fig. 6

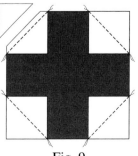

Fig. 9

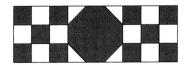

Fig. 7

Fig. 8

To make Flying Geese Units:

The following technique is used in several of the patterns in this book, (Fig. 10).

1.	Cut a rectangle the finished size required, plus seam allowances.

2.	Cut two squares one-half the length of the finished unit, plus seam allowances.

3.	Stitch one square in place, press it back to its corner and trim seam allowance to 1/8".

4.	Sew the other square on the other side the same way; the seams will "cross" at the seam allowance, making a perfect point. Press and trim as before, (Fig.11).

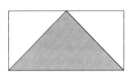

Fig. 10

Cutting Many Same-Size Pieces

An easy way to correctly cut many pieces of the same size is to tape drafting tape strips to the bottom of your cutting ruler precisely where you will line up the ruler to make the cuts. This method is great for faster cutting of many like pieces because you do not have to measure each time you make a cut. It also eliminates any cutting errors. Drafting tape is also great for marking your ruler to cut unusual shapes.

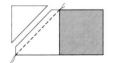 

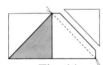

Fig. 11

Seam Allowance

To prevent bulky seams, which are unattractive and almost impossible to quilt through, a 1/8" seam allowance (finished size) is needed. Some quilters are most comfortable sewing a 1/4" seam allowance, as used for larger quilts; afterward, they trim each seam to 1/8". I find that double the effort. With experimentation and practice, it is not difficult to sew a 1/8" seam.

Here are some suggestions for achieving a perfect 1/8" seam. First, experiment with your machine's presser feet. The inside edge on the right side of your standard foot may be 1/8" from the seam line. Or the outside edge of the small straight stitch foot may be 1/8" from the seam line. If necessary, use a permanent marker to mark one foot precisely where it meets the edge of the fabric. If your machine has different needle positions, one combined with the right presser foot may be perfect. Even an edge-stitch foot or a blind-hem foot set correctly can make it a cinch. You may come up with more than one way to ensure success.

Now, if none of the above offers that perfect 1/8", do not despair! Take your square ruler marked with those perfect 1/8" lines and place it under your presser foot. Lower the needle gently onto the line that is 1/8" from the edge of the ruler. Anchor the ruler with tape so that it is straight. Very carefully place masking tape or drafting tape flush against the edge of the ruler. This tape guide is helpful even if a presser foot alone can give you a 1/8" seam.

Test the seam guide by cutting two strips of fabric 5/8" wide by 6" long. Sew the long sides together, using the seam guide. From the right side, press the 1/8" seam allowance to one side. Measure the width of the strip set. It should measure exactly 1" wide. If it is a scant narrower, relocate the tape a little closer to the needle. If it is a scant wider, relocate the tape a little farther from the needle. Keep in mind that the seam allowance must include the width of the seam line itself. When the guide is precisely located, you can build up several layers of tape to form a ridge, or use a single narrow strip of Moleskin. The ridge will keep your fabric straight as you sew.

If, after practicing sewing 1/8" seams, you find that it is not for you, you can adjust the patterns in this book for 1/4" seams by adding 1/4" to every piece.

Throat Plate

The size of the hole in a zig-zag plate allows the fabric to drop into the hole. Using a far-right needle position with a zig-zag plate helps eliminate this problem.

If you are using a center needle position to achieve your 1/8" seam allowance, you may also want to use a straight-stitch throat plate on your machine. This plate helps produce a very straight stitch. If a straight-stitch throat plate did not come with your machine, I recommend purchasing one.

Stitch Length

You will be using chain-piecing methods whenever possible, which means the seams will not be secured with a backstitch. Therefore, a short stitch length is necessary. I work at 14 stitches per inch. Do not go any shorter; the seam will be very difficult to take out in case of error. You will cross these seams with other seams, which will secure them.

Sew Slowly

Slow, controlled sewing is necessary to ensure perfect narrow seams. If your sewing machine has a slow speed setting, use that feature. If not, slow yourself down and become accustomed to it.

Butting Seams

In order to match seams when joining one unit to another, press the seam allowances in opposite directions, toward the darker fabric whenever possible. The seam allowances will butt each other at the seam line. This makes it easy to match the seams and it also distributes the bulk of the seam allowances. Occasionally, pressing a seam toward the darker fabric will not butt the seams; that seam should be pressed toward the light fabric.

Intersecting Seams

When approaching the intersection of more than two seams (as with triangles), pin through the point of the top fabric and through the point of the bottom fabric. Line up the points so they are straight on the pin and place another pin on either side of the positioning pin. Remove the positioning pin and stitch exactly through the intersection.

Chain Piecing

Think of mass production methods in garment factories. One person sews the same unit on many garments, assembly fashion. The same principle can be applied to quiltmaking. Piece the like units of the different blocks in assembly fashion to save time and thread. Sometimes one individual block has so many like pieces, you can piece them by this method, too, (Fig. 12).

Sew like units together in a chain by feeding pairs of units under the presser foot. Sew the first seam, add another pair, sew that seam, etc. Because of the size of our pieces, it is best to raise the presser foot each time and very carefully position pairs to achieve the accuracy you need for your seams. Clip units apart after you have completed the chain.

Do not worry about the seams coming apart. Remember you are using 14 stitches to the inch. Soon you will be crossing each of these seams with another seam, which will secure them.

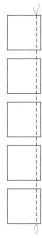

Fig. 12

The visual arrangement of the blocks in a quilt top is called the "set." The basic sets are straight and diagonal, (Fig. 13 & 14).

It is easy to figure the dimensions of a straight set quilt by simply multiplying the size of the block times the number of blocks in the width and in the length. If you have added sashing between the blocks, these widths will have to be added in, also.

Diagonal sets, where the blocks are set on point, take a bit more thought. You need to know the diagonal width of a block to do this.

FORMULA: Finished block size times 1.414 = diagonal width.

EXAMPLE: 3" finished block x 1.414 = 4.242 or 4 1/4".

Now it is simple to multiply the number of blocks times the diagonal width to find the dimensions of a diagonally set quilt.

Setting Triangles

Setting triangles are cut from a square. To determine the size of the square, add 1 1/4" to the diagonal width of the block. Using the diagonal width from the above example, you would add 1 1/4" to 4 1/4", resulting in a 5 1/2" square. The square is cut diagonally both ways to make (4) setting triangles. The straight grain follows the long edges, which helps keep the quilt "square."

These triangles are a little larger than exact size, which allows you to "float" the blocks, making them appear to lay on top of the background rather than meet the border. If you prefer that the blocks meet the border, simply even up the sides of the pieced area with a long ruler and rotary cutter, leaving a seam allowance.

Corners

To determine the size squares required for cutting corner triangles, add 1" to the finished block size.

FORMULA: Finished block size plus 1" = the size square to cut for making corner triangles.

For a 3" finished block you would cut (2) 4" squares in half diagonally to make the (4) corner triangles. Once again, the straight grain of the fabric will be on the outside edges of the quilt, but this time on the two shorter sides of the triangles.

Finger press a crease in the center of the corner triangle and in the center of the block that will be stitched to the corner triangle. Match the two creases and pin. Also pin the two edges, leaving an equal amount of triangle exposed on both sides. Stitch the seam and press. Repeat for all four corners. Using the square ruler, trim the corners even with the sides of the quilt.

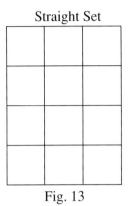

Straight Set

Fig. 13

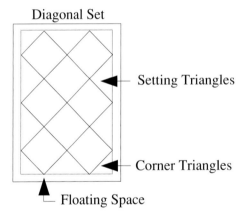

Diagonal Set

Setting Triangles

Corner Triangles

Floating Space

Fig. 14

BORDERS

Borders should enhance the beauty of your quilt. Borders that are too wide or too intricate can easily overpower the main quilt pattern. This is especially true for miniature quilts. I lay different fabrics along the sides of the quilt top to determine what I like best. The border fabric does not always have to be the same as one of the fabrics in the quilt, but it should be complementary. Sometimes a quilt top looks better without a border. Many strikingly beautiful antique quilts have no borders.

The easiest way to add borders is by the straight-cut corner method, (Fig. 15). First, measure the length of the quilt top through the center. Cut (2) border strips that measurement and sew to each side of the quilt. Press seams toward the border strips. Now measure the width of the quilt with its side borders, again through the center. Cut (2) border strips that measurement and sew to the top and bottom of the quilt. Additional borders of varying widths can be added in similar fashion.

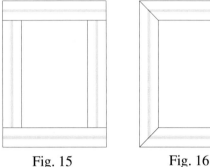

Fig. 15   Fig. 16

Some borders look more attractive when they are mitered at the corners, such as printed wallpaper-type stripes, (Fig. 16). The easiest method I have found for mitering corners is illustrated below.

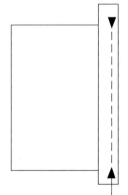

End stitching exactly 1/8" or 1/4" from ends. Depending on your seam allowance.

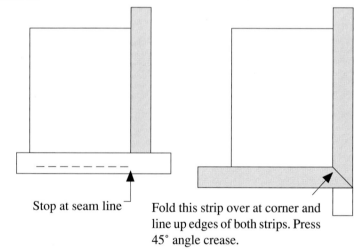

Stop at seam line

Fold this strip over at corner and line up edges of both strips. Press 45° angle crease.

Sew the seam on the crease, ending exactly at the point where the two seams stopped on the border strips. Check to see that it is a good miter. If not, remove the inaccurate stitches or add stitches to close the gap. Cut the seam allowance back to 1/4". Press this seam open.

If you desire several different mitered borders, it is easiest to first sew together the various strips into one border unit before mitering the corners, (Fig. 17). Now handle the unit as one border strip and miter the corners.

Fig. 17

Selecting Batting

Only very thin batting should be used in a miniature quilt, so it will fold and drape easily rather than be rigid. Some regular loft batts can be peeled into two layers, which makes them suitable for small quilts. If you use 100% cotton batting, quilt it every 1/2" to hold it in place. Cotton will also "beard." However, it will give your miniature quilt an antique appearance. After washing, cotton batting shrinks, causing a slightly puckered look.

Having experimented with all the top brands, my preference is to use a very thin polyester batting. Experiment with crib size batts to find your personal favorite. Just remember: Think thin!

Backing Fabric

If you used light fabrics in your quilt, do not use a dark fabric for the backing. It will show through the top and batting, changing the color of the light fabrics and sometimes causing shadows where the seam allowances lay. If you'd like your quilting stitches to show on the back, use a light solid color or muslin; if you'd rather they be camouflaged, use a print.

Because the quilting stitches sometimes cause the backing to draw up to a smaller size, cut your backing 1" to 1 1/2" larger on all sides than the quilt top. The excess will be trimmed after the binding is attached to the quilt top.

Basting

The easiest way to baste the layers of a miniature quilt together is to "pin baste." I use 1" safety pins. There are larger pins on the market, called quilter's safety pins, but they make holes in the fabric which are very noticeable in a tiny quilt. You do not need large safety pins because you are using thin batting and there is less bulk than with a large quilt. Do not use straight pins for basting. They will either get caught, come out or stab you!

Secure the quilt layers with safety pins in areas where you will not be quilting. (You can always remove a pin if it is in the way.) Remember to keep the quilt straight, both horizontally and vertically, and to keep it pucker-free as you pin it.

Marking Quilt Lines

If you wish to do intricate quilting on your miniature quilt, it is best to mark the top before you layer it. Mark very lightly with pencil or use a water soluble marking pen. You must be sure to remove every trace of this ink with cold water, or it may come back to haunt you, and may even harm the fabric. I sometimes mark quilting patterns, but more often I quilt "in the ditch" or near the seams, which does not require marking.

If you desire to add some quilted embellishments, cut small shapes from Contact® paper, remove the backing and stick the shape where you want it. Then quilt around it. It works very well; you can even move the Contact® paper to other areas.

To Hoop or Not To Hoop

If you are accustomed to quilting on a hoop, you will probably want to use one for miniatures, as well. The problem is, what size? Some quilts are too small for most hoops. and flimsy hoops designed for needlework will not hold a quilt very well.

My solution is to use a scroll-type needlework frame. The edges of the quilt top and backing are pinned to fabric strips which are fastened to the frame. An 11" x 17" Q-Snap plastic frame also works quite well. It is not necessary to fasten down the sides of the quilt on either of these frames. The tension is controlled by turning the rods. The principle is the same as a large floor frame.

The other alternative is not to use a hoop at all, which is my preference. My left hand pushes those little stitches onto the quilting needle in my right hand. They make a great team!

Hand Quilting or Machine Quilting

Personal preference is the biggest factor here. I machine quilt most of my larger quilts, but I enjoy hand quilting miniatures; it is very relaxing. Because they are small, you can quilt them anywhere. For machine quilting, use a fine nylon thread on the top of your machine and regular thread that matches the backing on the bobbin. A clear nylon thread is best for light fabrics; a darker, smoky color for darker fabrics. If possible, use a walking foot on your machine. A regular presser foot tends to push the top layer ahead of the others, causing puckers. The walking foot feeds all three layers under the needle at the same time.

Simply quilting in the ditch (between seams) is the easiest method for machine quilting, but intricate quilting can also be done by machine with a darning foot.

Binding

I prefer a 3/8" finished binding on my miniature quilts. The more traditional 1/2" width seems out of proportion to the size of the quilt. Bias binding is not necessary on quilts with straight sides.

Measure the outer edge of the quilt to determine the total length of binding needed. Then add about 6" more to allow for mitering the corners. On the crossgrain of the fabric, cut enough 2" wide strips to go around the quilt. Join the strips into one long piece by cutting the ends at a 45° angle and then sewing two angled edges together with a 1/4" seam. The seam will be almost unnoticeable, because the bulk is distributed evenly, (Fig.18).

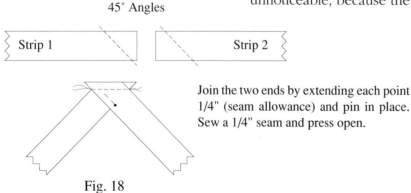

45° Angles

Strip 1   Strip 2

Join the two ends by extending each point 1/4" (seam allowance) and pin in place. Sew a 1/4" seam and press open.

Fig. 18

Press the long strip in half lengthwise, making a 1" wide double binding strip.

Before applying the binding to the quilt, pin the quilt's edges as illustrated. Using the walking foot, sew a narrow seam all around the edges. This will result in a smooth, pucker-free bound edge. I also find it helpful not to cut off any of the excess batting and backing until after I have machine-sewn the binding onto the quilt top, (Fig. 19).

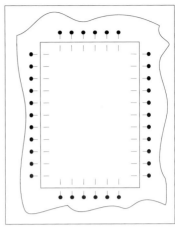

Fig. 19

Replace the walking foot with the regular presser foot. Starting about one-fourth of the way up from the bottom right, lay the raw edges of the binding on the raw edges of the quilt top, right sides together. Leave about 6" of the binding free behind the foot (for joining the ends later), and begin sewing a 1/4" seam down to the lower corner. Stop stitching exactly 1/4" from the corner edge. Leave the needle in the fabric, raise the presser foot and turn the quilt so that you are ready to stitch down the next edge. Backstitch off the edge instead of going forward. Fold the binding straight up, forming a 45° angle, and then make a second fold just above the top edge of the quilt. Make sure the folded edges on the left are exactly aligned. Begin stitching forward again through all thicknesses, (Fig. 20).

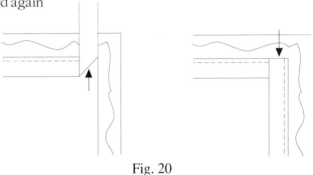

Fig. 20

Repeat this procedure for the next three corners. When you come back to the first side, stop stitching near the top of the quilt about one-fourth of the way down and backstitch. Remove the quilt from the machine and lay it on a flat surface. Lay the free ends of the binding along the unstitched portion of the quilt's edge and overlap them. Mark the left end with a pin at the quilt's midpoint. Open out the left end of the binding. Using the square ruler, cut a 45° angle at the pin mark, (Fig. 21). Refold the strip.

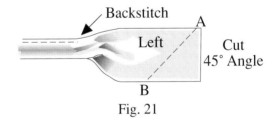

Fig. 21

Lay the unstitched left end over the right end. On the right end, mark points A and B with a dot, (Fig. 22).

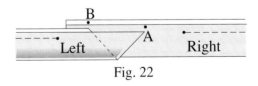

Fig. 22

Open out the right end. Measure and cut a 45° angle 1/2" to the *left* of the dots. Place the right sides of the two ends together and sew with a 1/4" seam allowance, (Fig. 18). Press the seam open and fold the joined strip in half. Press. Lay the unstitched portion of the binding on the edge of the quilt and finish stitching it to the quilt, (Fig. 23).

Now is the time to trim the excess batting and backing, about 1/4" from the edges of the quilt top. This allowance will fill the 3/8" binding completely. Wrap the binding over the edge to the back of the quilt. Place the folded edge of the binding on top

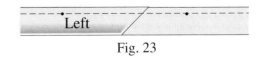

Fig. 23

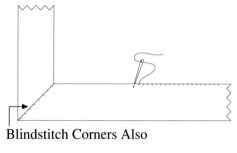

Blindstitch Corners Also

Fig. 24

of the stitching line and sew a tiny blindstitch to secure it. Your stitches should be no farther apart than 1/8".

The binding on the top of the quilt will already be mitered. On the back, fold the miter in the opposite direction from that on the front and secure it with tiny blindstitches, (Fig. 24).

Signing Your Quilts

Do sign your quilts on the back! Include your name, city and state, and the year. You might also record the name of the quilt, that of the recipient and the occasion for the quilt's presentation. You can embroider the information, type it on a piece of muslin and sew it to the backing, or create a counted cross-stitch label. Or simply use a special pen made for writing on fabric, one that will not bleed, wash out or fade. To stabilize fabric for writing, iron it to a piece of freezer paper. Remove the paper after the label has been made.

Caring for Your Completed Quilts

Spraying finished quilts with fabric protector will help keep dirt from penetrating the fibers of the fabrics. I use a soft bristle baby brush to remove lint and dust. If, at some time, a quilt requires laundering, simply wash it by hand in a basin of lukewarm water with mild soap. Let it soak a short while, then gently squeeze the suds through it. Do not wring the quilt; just gently squeeze out the excess water and soap. Rinse thoroughly several times until no soap remains. Roll the quilt in a towel to absorb excess water, then allow it to dry flat on a clean towel or sweater dryer. Your little quilts will look beautiful! If the fabrics were not washed prior to cutting and sewing, a little shrinking may occur, but this will only give your quilt a desirable antique look.

If you must store your quilts, do not use plastic. Place the quilts in cotton pillowcases; the natural fibers breathe, permitting air to circulate and preventing mildew. Quilts should be aired out occasionally, and also refolded to prevent permanent creases from forming.

With the proper care, your tiny treasures will become family heirlooms.

Patterns

12" Square
25 Blocks

This pattern dates from the early nineteenth century. Two templates were traditionally used, but these blocks are a breeze to make when three bias strips are first sewn together and then cut on the diagonal with a square ruler. Instant pieced blocks!

FABRIC REQUIREMENTS

Choose one fabric for the centers and three coordinating fabrics for the corner segments.

1/4 yard Fabric #1; used for 7 blocks.
1/4 yard Fabric #2; used for 12 blocks.
1/4 yard Fabric #3; used for 6 blocks.
1/4 yard Fabric #4 is used for the center segments of all 25 blocks. Choose muslin or a white on muslin print.
1/2 yard, Backing
1/4 yard, Border and Binding

CUTTING AND PIECING

1. Cut 1 1/2" wide bias strips:
Fabric #1 totaling about 54" long.
Fabric #2 totaling about 100" long.
Fabric #3 totaling about 50" long.
2. Cut 1" wide bias strips of Fabric #4 totaling about 102" long.
3. Sew these various strips lengthwise into three different set-ups, (Fig. 25). Press seams away from center.
4. Using the square ruler, cut 2" bias squares by aligning the diagonal line vertically on the center of the muslin section of the set-ups. Make sure that the 2" marks are level horizontally. Cut the required number of bias squares from each set-up. See illustration above and Cutting Instructions.

ASSEMBLY

1. Arrange the 25 squares according to the photograph. Proper color placement is essential to the design.
2. First Border: Cut one 5/8" x 44" strip of contrasting fabric. Subcut to fit and stitch to quilt using straight-cut corner method.
3. Second Border: Cut two 1 3/4" wide strips of desired fabric. Subcut to the lengths needed and stitch to quilt, using the straight-cut corners method.
4. Layer the quilt with batting and backing. Quilt and bind as desired.

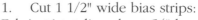

1 3/4" Finished Block

Fig. 25

HUNTER'S STAR

14 1/2" x 19"
24 Blocks

Notice the bright LeMoyne stars that are formed by the careful placement of the blocks. A minimum of 16 or 24 blocks is required to make the design work out.

FABRIC REQUIREMENTS
1/4 yard light
1/8 yard accent
1/4 yard dark
3/8 yard, second border and binding
5/8 yard, backing

CUTTING
Light Fabric
1.   Cut (1) 2 5/16" x 44" strip. Cut into (12) 2 5/16" squares. Cut each square diagonally, making (24) triangles.
2.   Cut (2) 3/4" x 44" strips. Keep strips folded in half. Cut a 45° angle on the left end. Measure over 2 3/4" and mark. Cut a 45° angle in the reverse direction from that mark. You need (24) trapezoids, so cut (12) double sets (Fig. 26).
3.   Cut (2) 3/4" x 44" strips. Keep strips folded in half. Cut a 45° angle on the left end. Place 3/4" line of ruler on the 45° angled cut edge and make next cut. You need (48) diamonds, so cut (24) double sets (Fig. 27).

Accent Fabric:
Cut (48) diamonds the same as you did for No. 3 under Light Fabric.

Dark Fabric:
1.   Cut (1) 2 5/16" x 44" strip. Cut into (12) 2 5/16" squares. Cut each square diagonally, making (24) triangles.
2.   Cut (24) trapezoids from dark fabric the same as you did for No. 2 under Light Fabric.

PIECING
1.   Chain-piece accent fabric diamonds to light fabric trapezoids. Press seams toward diamonds, (Fig. 28 & 29).
2.   Chain-piece light fabric diamonds to dark fabric trapezoids. Press seams toward trapezoids.

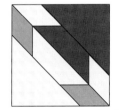

2 1/2" Finished Blocks

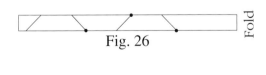

Fig. 26

Fig. 27

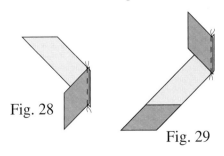

Fig. 28

Fig. 29

25

3.   Sew these two units together along the longest edges. Press seams toward dark trapezoids (Fig. 30).
4.   Sew large triangles to appropriate trapezoid. Be extremely careful to pin centers and ends exactly (Fig. 31).

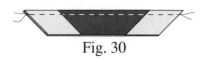

Fig. 30

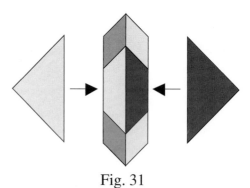

Fig. 31

ASSEMBLY
1.   Arrange blocks according to photograph and stitch together.
2.   First Border: Cut (2) 3/4" x 44" strips of accent fabric. Subcut to fit and stitch to quilt using straight-cut corner method.
3.   Second Border: Cut (2) 2" x 44" strips of dark fabric. Subcut to fit and stitch to quilt.
4.   Layer quilt with batting and backing. Quilt and bind as desired.

TREE OF LIFE

14" x 19"

This traditional quilt design is one of my favorites. The early "quilting" settlers in our country were inspired by the Bible in much of their work. Revelation 22:14 says, "Blessed are they that do his commandments, that they may have the right to the tree of life..."

FABRIC REQUIREMENTS
5/8 yard for main fabric and binding
1 yard for background and backing

CUTTING
The number given in parentheses is for making six blocks from the same fabrics. If you desire to make different blocks, use the first number for each block.
1.   Cut 24 (144) 3/4" bias squares of a main fabric and background fabric combination. Refer to the section on making bias squares.
2.   Cut 4 (24) half-square triangles of main fabric by first cutting 2 (12) 15/16" squares and then cutting them in half diagonally.
3.   Cut 2 (12) half-square triangles of background fabric by first cutting 1 (6) 1 7/16" squares and then cutting them in half diagonally.
4.   Cut 3 (18) 3/4" squares of background fabric.
5.   Trunk Squares:
    a. Cut 1 7/8" wide bias strips of background fabric totaling 24". Subcut into (12) 1 7/8" lengths.
    b. Cut a rectangle of main fabric 1 7/8" x 3 3/4". Subcut (6) 5/8" x 1 7/8" strips (for trunks) from rectangle.
    c. Sew (1) trunk strip between (2) bias background strips. Make six of these units.
    d. Cut (12) 1 1/4" wide bias strips of tree fabric, each 4" long.
    e. Sew the 1 1/4" bias strips to the top and bottom of each set-up.

3 1/2" Finished Block

    f. Using the square ruler, cut a 2 1/4" square from each of the above set-ups by aligning the diagonal line on the center of the trunk strip, with the 1 1/4" side markings on the top seam line. Cut off the top two angles. Reverse square ruler and cut the 2 1/4" square.

PIECING
Chain-piece the following units for each block in sequence, (Fig. 32). Make the number of units given in

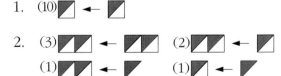

Fig. 32

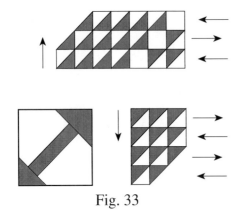

Fig. 33

parentheses. After each sequence, remove the chain from the sewing machine and clip the units apart. It is easiest to wait until you finish all the steps to press all the seam allowances to the dark fabric at the same time.

Assemble all these rows and trunk square as in block illustration. Add two corners last. Press seams in direction of arrows (Fig. 33).

ASSEMBLY

1. Center Squares: Cut (2) 3 3/4" squares of background fabric.
2. Setting Triangles: Cut (2) 6 1/4" squares of background fabric and cut both ways diagonally. Need (6).
3. Corner Triangles: Cut (2) 4 1/2" squares of background fabric and cut in half diagonally. Need (4).
4. Assemble quilt.
5. First Border: Cut (2) 5/8" x 44" strips of main fabric and subcut to fit. Stitch to quilt using straight-cut corner method.
6. Second Border: Cut (2) 2" x 44" strips of background fabric and subcut to fit. Stitch to quilt using straight-cut corner method.
7. Layer quilt with batting and backing. Quilt as desired.
9. Bind with same fabric as first border.

POINSETTIA BASKET

15" Square

This is a modified version of the traditional "North Carolina Lily" pattern. Instead of using four diamonds for each flower with set-in background pieces, I have used a simplified sew-and-cut method to make a similar flower. Also, the stems are pieced rather than appliqued. This little quilt makes a lovely Christmas wallhanging; different colors could make it a "May Basket."

FABRIC REQUIREMENTS

1/4 yard each fabric for flowers and green
1/8 yard for baskets
1/2 yard for background and backing
1/4 yard for first border and binding
1/8 yard for second border

CUTTING AND PIECING

Letters correspond to those on the block diagram.
A/B Triangle Unit: Total (12)
1.   Cut 1" wide bias strips of red fabric and green fabric, totaling about 30" each. Sew similar lengths of red and green strips together into pairs. Press seams toward green fabric. Turn strips so that the red fabric is on the bottom. Place square ruler with the 7/8" line markings on the seam line. The point of the ruler is on the green fabric. Cut the top two angles, (Fig. 34).
2.   Now turn the cut triangle with the point facing downwards and make a straight cut across the red fabric, 9/16" from the seam line, (Fig. 35).

C/D Triangle Unit: Total (24)
    Cut 1" wide bias strips of red fabric and background fabric, totaling about 25". Sew similar lengths of red and background strips together into pairs. Press seams toward the red fabric. With red fabric on the left side, make a straight cut across bottom. Cut (12) triangles by placing diagonal line of square ruler on seam line, with the 1 1/16" line markings on the bottom cut edge. Cut the two angles. Make another straight cut and repeat the procedure. You need (12) triangles with the red triangle on the left. Turn the bias strip unit so that the background fabric is on the left. Using the same cutting procedure, cut (12) triangles with the background triangle on the left, (Fig. 36).

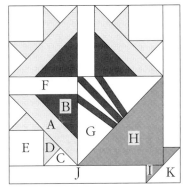

3 1/2" Finished Block

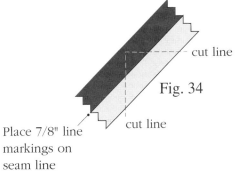

Place 7/8" line markings on seam line

cut line
cut line

Fig. 34

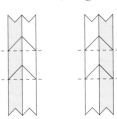

Fig. 36

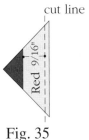

cut line

Red 9/16"

Fig. 35

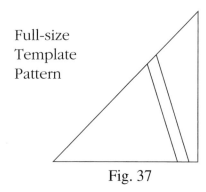

Full-size
Template
Pattern

Fig. 37

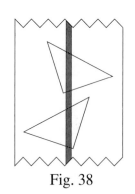

Fig. 38

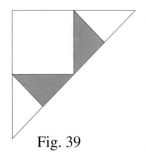

Fig. 39

E.   Cut (12) 7/8" squares of background fabric.
F.   Cut (8) 3/4" x 1 1/2" rectangles of background fabric.
G.   Triangle and three stems unit: Total (4)
1.   Cut a 1 1/2" wide strip of background fabric on the straight grain, about 28" long. Divide in half.
2.   Cut a 3/8" x 44" strip of green fabric. Cut off a 14" length.
3.   Sew the green strip between the two background strips. Press seams to background fabric.
4.   On template plastic, trace triangle pattern, including the stem lines, (Fig. 37). Align the template on the strip set-up and cut out (4) left-side stem triangles. Flip template to other side and cut out (4) right-side triangles, (Fig. 38).
5.   Take remaining portion of green strip and stitch between the right and left stem triangles to form the three-stem unit. Cut the center stem strip off a little higher than the two triangle sides. Press seams of center stem to outside.
H.   Cut (2) 2 3/16" squares of basket fabric. Cut each diagonally to make (4) basket triangles.
I.   Cut (4) 15/16" squares of basket fabric. Cut each triangle diagonally to make (8) small basket triangles.
J.   Cut (1) 3/4" x 44" strip of background fabric. Subcut into (8) 3/4" x 2 3/4" strips.
K.   Cut (2) 1 7/16" squares of background fabric and cut once diagonally to make (4) triangles.

ASSEMBLY
1.   Make (12) units like this, (Fig. 39).
2.   Stitch the above (12) units to bottom flower triangles (A/B).
3.   Stitch entire block together. Be sure to align stem seams correctly.
4.   Center Square: Cut (1) 3 3/4" square of background fabric.
5.   Setting Triangles: Cut (1) 6 1/4" square of background fabric and cut diagonally both ways to make (4) triangles.
6.   Corners: Cut (2) 4 1/2" squares of background fabric and cut in half diagonally to make (4) corners.
7.   Assemble quilt as illustrated.
8.   First Border: Cut (2) 5/8" x 44" strips of red fabric. Subcut to fit and stitch to quilt using straight-cut corner method.
9.   Second Border: Cut (2) 2" x 44" strips of contrasting fabric. Subcut to fit and stitch to quilt using straight-cut corner method.
10. Layer quilt with batting and backing. Quilt and bind as desired.

Challenge of the Unknown Stars. *7" x 9". Sewing the larger units and cutting them to a smaller size simplifies piecing these 1 1/2" star blocks. Easy Four-Patch units give the illusion of sashing. Pattern, page 61.*

Star Light, Star Bright. *A dozen 2 1/8" stars in strong contemporary prints float in a swirling print background. Snowball blocks link them together. Pattern, page 64.*

Spinning Pinwheels. *9 1/2" x 12 1/2". Strip set-ups mean working with small squares rather than tiny triangles. The backgrounds are the same in a dozen blocks with different colored pinwheels. Blue setting triangles make an instant border. Pattern, page 54.*

Lexington Strippy Quilt. *13 3/4" x 19". This quilt consists of seven "strips." Rows of seven Nine-Patch blocks alternate with rows cut from a border print. A strip across the top and bottom completes the design with self-borders. Pattern, page 56.*

Twisting Star*. 12" x 16". These stars, with points that appear to overlap each other at their bases, are easily pieced from quick-cut triangles and octagons. Place dark fabrics in these positions and float the stars on a light background for a sparkling effect. Pattern, page 50.*

33

Hunter's Star. *14 1/2" x 19". This simple block comes to life when 24 of them are pieced together. LeMoyne Stars appear to float in the center of larger Pinwheel blocks. The diamonds, triangles and trapezoids are easily cut with precision from strips. Pattern, page 25.*

Tree of Life. *14" x 19". Working with bias strip set-ups keeps everything on the straight and narrow, especially the tiny triangle units. Don't worry if the points don't match up perfectly every time. Your quilt will still be wonderful! Pattern, page 27.*

I Love the USA. *11 1/2" x 16". The star points are made with connector squares, which are also used to round off the tops of the hearts. Connector squares eliminate handling of bias edges on triangles and insure the block's success. Pattern, page 45.*

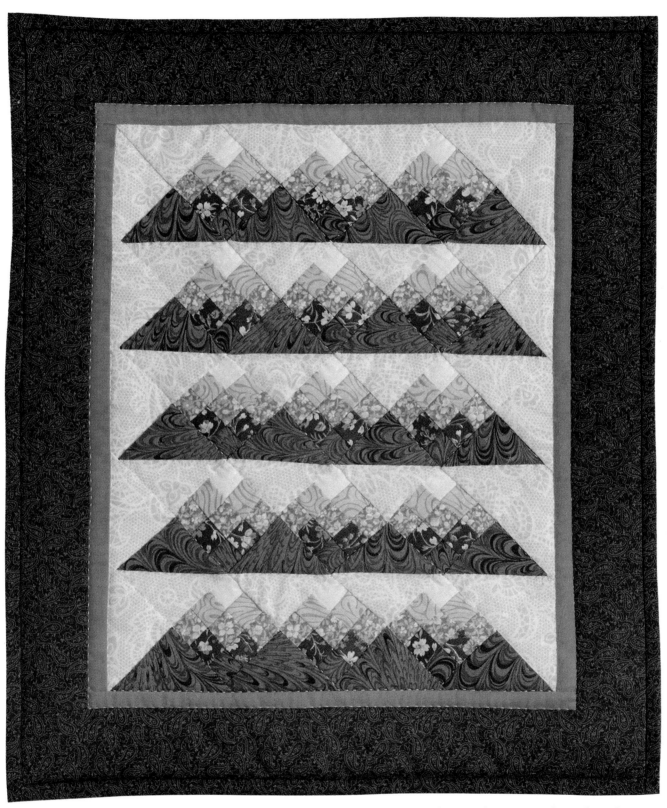

Rocky Mountain Splendor. *12 1/2" x 14 1/2". Mountains are made out of Nine-Patches when they are rotated a quarter-turn. Three strip set-ups make fifteen blocks. Fabrics are chosen to represent snowy peaks and forested foothills; purples reinforce the image of mountains. Pattern, page 43.*

Little Blue Houses. 11 1/2" x 15". These 3" house blocks are traditional in design, but they are thoroughly modern and easy to make with strip set-ups and a 60° ruler. Pattern, page 48.

California Star. 13" x 13". Use two colors as shown or substitute a third color in the large triangles of the star points and portions of the central block. Bias squares make easy work of the triangle units. Pattern, page 52.

Indian Hatchets. 12" x 12". This tiny treasure consists of twenty-five blocks which are cut in their entirety from three different strip set-ups. Show off some of your favorite fabrics! Pattern, page 24.

Poinsettia Basket. 15" x 15". A modified version of the North Carolina Lily, the stems are pieced rather than appliquéd—it's easier than you think! Make it as shown for Christmas, or in spring colors for a May Basket. Pattern, page 29.

Delectable Mountain Lakes. 14" x 14". Blue in the central areas of this traditional Delectable Mountains arrangement gives the pattern a new look. Hand-dyed fabric with a slightly mottled appearance creates watery lakes. Make quick-pieced squares from bias strips for a quick-and-easy miniature quilt. Pattern, page 60.

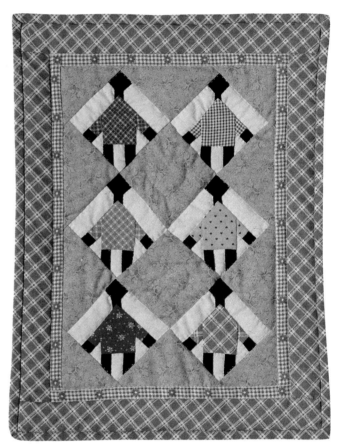

Southern Mammy Quilt. 10 1/2" x 13 1/2". Variations of this pattern have been handed down from the slaves of the pre-Civil War days. No-template techniques make the 2 1/2" block much easier to piece. Pattern, page 58.

Cat Crossing. *15 1/2" x 16 1/2".* A cat's a cat, and that's that! And just like a cat, there's more to this pattern than meets the eye. Use four different fabrics for four cats, or use the same fabric in each block to show one cat in four poses. Personalize the block patterns to show off your cat's colors by adding patches in just the right places! Pattern, page 39.

CAT CROSSING

15 1/2" x 16 1/2"

Cats are some of my favorite people, so I designed a cat wallhanging to make my cats and me happy. If you like cats, try making this little quilt. If you do not like cats, give them a chance to win you over, and then make this little quilt!

The connector square method makes these cats easy to piece. There are separate instructions for each cat. Make one cat in different poses by using all the same fabrics, or make four different cats.

FABRIC REQUIREMENTS
1/8 yard of each cat fabric
1/2 yard background and backing
1/8 yard accent border
1/4 yard main border and binding

CAT No. 1, Sitting Front View
Unit I
A.   Cut a rectangle 1 3/4" x 1 1/4" of cat fabric.
B.   Cut (2) 3/4" squares of cat fabric.
C.   Cut a rectangle 3/4" x 1 3/4" of background fabric.
Connect B squares to the C rectangle, (Fig. 40). Trim.
D.   Cut a rectangle 1 3/4" x 2 3/4" of background fabric.
Assemble Unit I (A/B/C/D).

Unit II
E.   Cut a rectangle 2 3/4" x 3 3/4" of cat fabric.
F.   Cut a rectangle 1" x 3 3/4" of cat fabric.
G.   Cut (2) 1" squares of white fabric for neck.
Connect a G square to the upper right corner of E
and a G square to the upper left corner of F. Trim.
H.   Cut a 2" square of background fabric. Connect this to
the upper left corner of E. Assemble Unit II (E/F/G/H).

Unit III
I.   Cut a rectangle 5/8" x 1" of cat fabric for tail.
J.   Cut a strip 5/8" x 3" of cat fabric for tail.
K.   Cut a rectangle 5/8" x 1" of white fabric for end of tail.
L.   Cut a strip 5/8" x 3" of background fabric. Assemble
Unit III (I/J/K/L).
Sew Units I, II and III together.
M.   Sashes: Cut (2) strips 3/4" x 5 1/4" of background fabric.
Sew one strip on each side of the block.
N.   Cut (1) strip 1 1/4" x 5 1/4" of background fabric and
stitch to the bottom of the block.

CAT NO. 2, Sitting Side View
Unit I
A.   Cut a rectangle of cat fabric 2" x 1 3/4".
B.   Cut a 3/4" square of cat fabric.

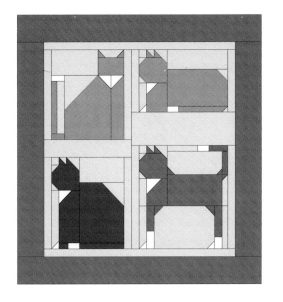

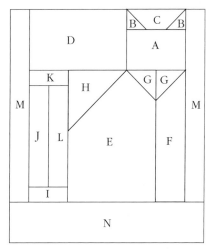

CAT No. 1, Sitting Front View

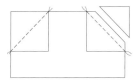

Fig. 40

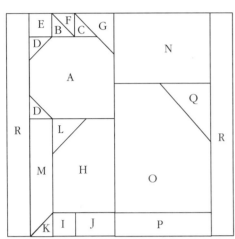

CAT NO. 2, Sitting Side View

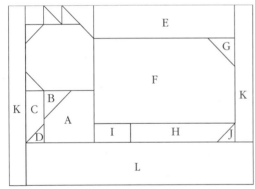

CAT NO. 3, Sleeping Side View

C.   Cut a 3/4" x 1" rectangle of cat fabric.
D.   Cut (2) 3/4" squares of background fabric. Connect these squares to the left corners of the A rectangle. Trim.
E.   Cut a 3/4" square of background fabric.
F.   Cut a 3/4" square of background fabric. Place B and F squares right sides together and sew a diagonal seam. Press cat fabric to corner and trim seam allowance back to 1/8". Sew E, B/F and C together. Sew this top section to the bottom section of this unit.
G.   Cut a 1" square of background fabric. Connect this square to the upper right corner of this unit. Assemble Unit I (A/B/C/D/E/F/G).

Unit II
H.   Cut a rectangle 1 1/2" x 2 7/8" of cat fabric.
I.   Cut a rectangle 5/8" x 3/4" of cat fabric.
J.   Cut a rectangle 1" x 5/8" of white fabric for tail end.
K.   Cut a 3/4" square of white fabric for paw.
L.   Cut a 1" square of contrast fabric for neck. Connect square to upper left corner of H. Trim.
M.   Cut a 3/4" x 3 1/4" strip of background fabric. Connect K square to lower right corner of M. Assemble Unit II (H/I/J/K/L/M).

Unit III
N.   Cut a rectangle 2 1/2" x 1 3/4" of background fabric.

Unit IV
O.   Cut a rectangle 2 1/2" x 3 3/8" of cat fabric.
P.   Cut a 5/8" x 2 1/2" strip of cat fabric. Sew to bottom of O.
Q.   Cut a 1 1/2" square of background fabric. Connect this square to the upper right corner of O. Assemble Unit IV (O/P/Q).
Sew the four units together.
R.   Sashes: Cut (2) 3/4" x 5 1/4" strips of background fabric and sew to sides of block.

CAT NO. 3, Sleeping Side View
Unit I
Construct the same as Cat No. 2, Unit I.

Unit II
A.   Cut a rectangle 1 1/2" x 1 3/4" of cat fabric.
B.   Cut a 1" square of white fabric. Connect this square to the upper left corner of A. Trim.
C.   Cut a strip 3/4" x 1 3/4" of background fabric.
D.   Cut a 3/4" square of white fabric for paw. Connect this square to the lower right corner of C. Trim. Assemble Unit II (A/B/C/D).

Unit III
E.   Cut a rectangle 1 1/4" x 3 3/4" of background fabric.
F.   Cut a rectangle 2 1/4" X 3 3/4" of cat fabric.

40

G.　Cut a 1" square of background fabric. Connect this square to upper right corner of F. Trim.

H.　Cut a strip 5/8" x 3" of cat fabric.

I.　Cut a rectangle 5/8" x 1" of white fabric for tail end.

J.　Cut a 5/8" square of background fabric. Connect this square to right end of tail. Trim. Assemble Unit III (E/F/G/H/I/J).

Sew the three units together.

K.　Sashes: Cut (2) strips 3/4" x 3 3/4" of background fabric and sew to sides of block.

L.　Cut (1) strip 2" x 6 1/2" of background fabric and sew to bottom of block. (Option: Cut this strip of 14-count Aida cloth and cross stitch "A Cat's A Cat And That's That!", (Fig. 41)).

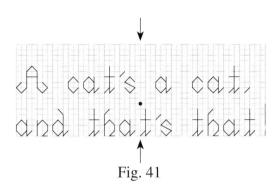

Fig. 41

Cat No. 4, Standing Side View

Unit I

Construct the same as Cat No. 2, Unit I.

Unit II

A.　Cut a rectangle 1 1/2" x 1 3/4" of cat fabric.

B.　Cut a 1" square of white fabric. Connect this square to the upper left corner of A. Trim.

C.　Cut a strip 3/4" x 1 3/4" of background fabric. Assemble Unit II (A/B/C).

Unit III

D.　Cut a rectangle 3 3/8" x 1 5/8" of background fabric.

E.　Cut a strip 5/8" x 1 3/4" of background fabric.

F.　Cut a strip 5/8" x 1" of white fabric for tail end.

G.　Cut a strip 5/8" x 1 1/2" of cat fabric for tail.

H.　Cut a strip 5/8" x 1 5/8" of cat fabric for tail.

I.　Cut a 3/4" square of cat fabric.

J.　Cut a 5/8" square of cat fabric. Connect the I square to the lower left corner of D and the J square to the lower right corner of D. Trim. Assemble Unit III (D/E/F/G/H/I/J).

Unit IV

K.　Cut a rectangle 3 3/8" x 2" of cat fabric.

L.　Cut a strip 5/8" x 2" of background fabric.

M.　Cut a 5/8" square of cat fabric and connect it to the upper left corner of L. Trim. Assemble Unit IV (K/L/M).

Unit V

N.　Cut a rectangle 2 1/2" x 3 5/8" of background fabric.

O.　Cut a strip 3/4" x 2 1/2" of background fabric.

P.　Cut a strip 3/4" x 1 1/2" of cat fabric.

Q.　Cut a strip 3/4" x 1 1/4" of white fabric for front leg.

R.　Cut (2) 5/8" squares of white fabric for paws. Connect one of these squares to the lower right corner of O and the other to the lower right corner of N. Trim.

S.　Cut a 3/4" x 1 3/4" strip of cat fabric.

T.　Cut a strip 3/4" x 1" of white fabric for back leg.

U.　Cut a strip 5/8" x 2 1/2" of background fabric.

V.　Cut (1) 3/4" square of cat fabric and connect it to the

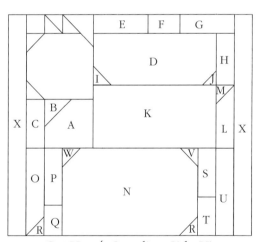

Cat No. 4, Standing Side View

upper right corner of N. Trim.

W.　Cut a 5/8" square of cat fabric and connect it to the upper left corner of N. Trim. Assemble Unit V (N through W). Sew the five units together.

X.　Sashes: Cut (2) strips 3/4" x 6" of background fabric. Sew one strip on each side of block.

ASSEMBLY

Quilt Top

1.　Arrange cat blocks as illustrated and stitch together.
2.　Cut (2) 11 1/4" x 3/4" strips of background fabric and sew to top and bottom of quilt top.

Borders

1.　Cut (2) 2" x 12 1/4" strips of border fabric and stitch to top and bottom using straight-cut corner method.
2.　Cut (2) 2" x 14" strips of border fabric and stitch to sides using straight-cut corner method.
3.　Layer quilt with batting and backing. Quilt and bind as desired.

quilt shown on page 35 # ROCKY MOUNTAIN SPLENDOR

12 1/2" x 14 1/2"

The mountains became very special to me when I lived in Colorado for about four years. This little quilt reminds me of their majestic beauty. In my travels, I saw a large quilt with Nine-Patch mountains, which inspired me to design this miniature quilt.

FABRIC REQUIREMENTS

Good color choices are essential to the design of this quilt. Visualize mountains in the distance, with a hazy, purple look. The main part of the quilt requires six different fabrics:
1/4 yard Fabric 1: Green for the base of the mountains
1/8 yard Fabric 2: Darker purple with green print
1/8 yard Fabric 3: Lavender print
1/8 yard Fabric 4: Misty mauve
1/8 yard Fabric 5: White for snow-capped peaks
1/4 yard Fabric 6: Pale blue for the sky
1/8 yard first border
1/4 yard second border and binding
1/2 yard backing

CUTTING

1.   There are (15) Nine-Patch blocks. Cut the following 3/4" wide strips, each 18" long:

1 strip of fabric #1
2 strips of fabric #2
3 strips of fabric #3
2 strips of fabric #4
1 strip of fabric #5

Carefully sew these strips into (3) different set-ups. Press the seams of Rows 1 and 3 toward the center and the seams of Row 2 away from the center, (Fig. 42). Subcut each set-up into (15) 3/4" segments. Sew these segments into (15) Nine-Patch blocks.

2.   There are (16) 1 3/4" bias squares to be used as alternating blocks with the Nine-Patch blocks. Cut 1 1/2" wide bias strips of the No. 1 fabric (mountain base) and No. 6 fabric (sky), totaling about 45". Seam the bias strips together, and press seams to dark fabric. Using the square ruler, cut (16) 1 3/4" squares.

15 Blocks   16 Blocks

1 1/2" Finished Blocks

Row 1	Row 2	Row 3
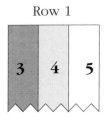	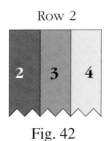	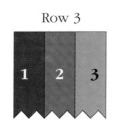

Fig. 42

3.   There are (18) setting triangles.
      a. Cut (4) 3 1/2" squares of Fabric No. 6 (sky) and cut both ways diagonally. You need (14) of these triangles.
      b. Cut (1) 3 1/2" square of Fabric No. 1 (green) and cut both ways diagonally for (4) triangles.

ASSEMBLY
1.   Assemble this diagonally-set quilt as illustrated. It is important that the bottom "rows" contain the green setting triangles. For the corner triangles, sew the short sides of two setting triangles together. Note that the two bottom corners are different from the top two corners.
2.   First Border: Cut (2) 5/8" x 44" strips of desired fabric. Subcut to fit and stitch to the quilt using straight-cut corner method.
3.   Second Border: Cut (2) 1 3/4" x 44" strips of desired fabric. Subcut to fit and stitch to the quilt.
4.   Layer the quilt with batting and backing. Quilt and bind as desired.

I LOVE THE USA

11 1/2" x 16" Square

These little pieced hearts are put together quickly, using connector squares to round out the tops of the hearts and to make the points of the stars. You can make all your hearts with stars inside, or you can fill them with pre-printed "USA" stripes, 16 squares, flags or whatever you choose. Options are given in the instructions.

FABRIC REQUIREMENTS
Scraps for star blocks
3/8 yard medium dark background and binding
1/2 yard backing

CUTTING FOR ONE STAR-IN-HEART BLOCK
Heart Fabric, Red
Cut a 1" wide strip 9" long and subcut:
A. (2) 1 3/4" x 1" rectangles.
B. (4) 5/8" x 1" rectangles.
C. (4) 5/8" squares.

Star Fabric, Blue
Cut a 1" wide strip 7" long and subcut:
D. (1) 1" square.
E. (8) 5/8" squares.

Background Fabric, Light
Cut a 1" wide strip 6" long and subcut:
F. (4) 5/8" squares.
G. (1) 1" square.

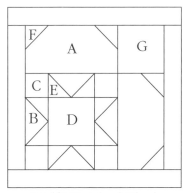

2 1/4" Finished Block

PIECING
1.   Stitch E squares to B rectangles by placing E on top of B as illustrated, (Fig. 43). Chain-piece all (4) rectangles on same side. Clip apart. Press squares to corners. Trim seam allowances to 1/8". Reverse sides of rectangles and chain-piece the other squares the same way. Press and trim seam allowances.
2.   Chain-piece in the following sequence:

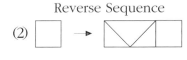

Reverse Sequence

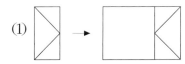

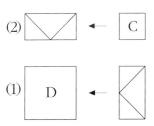

Clip apart and press top unit seam allowance toward square and bottom toward large center square.

Clip and press as before.

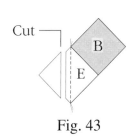

Cut

Fig. 43

45

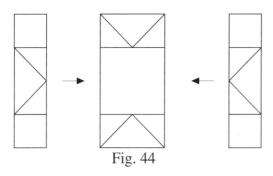

Fig. 44

3. Stitch these units together to make a star, (Fig. 44).
4. Stitch F squares to A rectangles, (Fig. 45).
5. Following the block illustration, sew one of the above units to the top of star unit. Press seam toward heart top. Sew a G square to left side of the other above unit and press seam toward heart. Now sew the remaining seam.
6. In order to provide enough distance between hearts on your diagonally-set quilt, sew a sashing around each block. Cut a 5/8" x 44" strip of background fabric and sew to all four edges of the heart blocks, trimming off excess as you go.

OPTIONAL BLOCKS AND CENTER VARIATIONS
NOTE: All of the optional blocks also need sashing strips sewn to them as described in No. 6 of the piecing instructions.
Cut (2) 1 3/4" x 1" rectangles of heart fabric, (4) 5/8" squares of background fabric, and (1) 1" square of background fabric. Use any of the following options for the center 1 3/4" diagonal square.
Stripes: Cut (5) 3/4" wide strips of different "USA" prints, each 2 3/4" long. Sew strips together side by side. Press seams all in the same direction. Place square ruler with its diagonal line centered on the fabric strips and cut a 1 3/4" diagonal square.

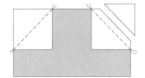

Fig. 45

Sixteen squares: Cut (8) 5/8" x 2" long strips. Sew (4) pairs of strips. Subcut each pair into (2) 5/8" segments. Mix these pairs randomly into the 16-square unit.

Square within a square (center square can be any design): Cut a 1 1/4" square for the center. Cut (2) 1 1/2" squares of desired fabric and cut each square in half diagonally. Sew (2) triangles to opposite sides of the square by matching centers. Press seams toward the center square.

Stitch the other (2) triangles to remaining sides. Press seams away from center square. Now align the diagonal line of the square ruler on the unit and cut a 1 3/4" diagonal square.

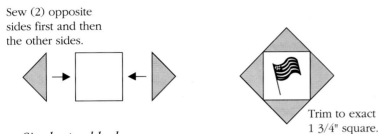

Sew (2) opposite sides first and then the other sides.

Trim to exact 1 3/4" square.

Single star block:
1. Cut (8) 13/16" squares of star fabric.
2. Cut (1) 1 3/8" square of star fabric.
3. Cut (4) 13/16" x 1 3/8" rectangles of background fabric.
4. Cut (4) 13/16" squares of background fabric.
5. Assemble single star block the same way as you would for the smaller star block inside the heart.

ASSEMBLY
1. Setting Triangles: Cut (2) 5 1/2" squares of dark background fabric and cut both ways diagonally. (Need 6.)
2. Corners: Cut (2) 4" squares of dark background fabric and cut each in half diagonally for (4) triangles.
3. Assemble quilt as illustrated.
4. First Border: Cut (1) 1/2" x 44" strip of an accent fabric. Subcut to fit and stitch to quilt using straight-corner method.
5. Second Border: Cut (2) 1 1/2" x 44" strips of dark background fabric. Subcut these strips to fit and stitch to quilt using straight-cut corner method.
6. Layer quilt with batting and backing. Quilt and bind as desired.

LITTLE BLUE HOUSES

11 1/2" x 15"

This is another favorite traditional design. You will not need any templates to cut the roof section, but your ruler must have a 60° angle line.

FABRIC REQUIREMENTS
1/2 yard main fabric
1/2 yard background and backing

CUTTING AND PIECING
Chimney Section, (Fig. 46)
A.　Cut (2) 3/4" x 6" strips of background fabric.
B.　Cut (2) 5/8" x 6" strips of main fabric.
C.　Cut (1) 1 1/2" x 6" strip of background fabric.
Sew strips together as illustrated and subcut into (6) 5/8" segments.

Roof Section, (Fig. 47)
A.　Cut a 1 1/8" wide strip of main fabric about 18" long. Align ruler and cut a 60° angle at left end of the strip. Make (6) cuts parallel to the 60° angle every 1 7/8", (Fig. 48).
B.　Cut a 1 1/4" wide strip of main fabric about 7" long. Align the 60° angle with the bottom edge of the strip, and cut angle toward the right at the top edge of the strip. Reverse the ruler and cut a 60° angle meeting the top point of the first cut. Cut (6), (Fig. 49).
C.　Cut a 3/4" x 12" strip of background fabric. Stitch this strip to the right side of the B triangle, leaving an extension at the top and bottom of the triangle. Press the seam toward the triangle. Trim the strip to 1/4" from the seam. Stitch the A parallelogram to the strip very carefully, and press this seam toward the parallelogram. Now trim the strip extensions at the top and bottom.
D.　Cut a rectangle 1 1/2" x 6" of background fabric. Divide into (6) rectangles 1 1/2" x 7/8", (Fig. 50). Cut (3) of these rectangles diagonally in one direction and the other (3) in the opposite direction. Stitch these triangles to the roof sections.

3" Finished Block

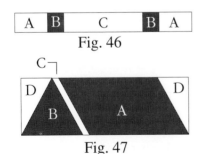

Fig. 46

Fig. 47

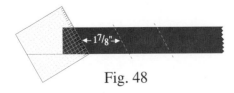

Fig. 48

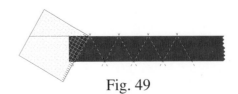

Fig. 49

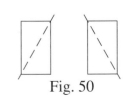

Fig. 50

Right House Section, (Fig. 51)

A.   Cut (3) 5/8" wide strips of main fabric, each 9" long. Cut (2) 5/8" wide strips of background fabric, 9" long. Sew strips together as in the A segment of the illustration, and subcut into 1 1/8" wide units.

B.   Cut (1) 5/8" x 27" strip of main fabric. Subcut into (12) 2 1/8" lengths. Sew to top and bottom of above set-ups.

C.   Cut (1) 3/4" x 27" strip of background fabric. Subcut (6) 2 1/8" segments and sew to top of each set-up. Press seams toward dark fabric. Trim each strip to 1/4" from seam. Next, subcut (6) 2" segments from strip and sew to left side of each set-up. Press seams toward dark fabric. Trim each strip to 1/4" from seam.

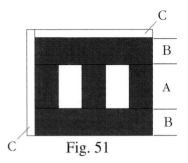

Fig. 51

Left House Section, (Fig. 52)

A.   Cut a 9/16" x 20" strip of main fabric. Divide in half.

B.   Cut a 5/8" x 10" strip of background fabric. Sew the A and B strips together and subcut (6) 1 1/2" segments.

C.   Cut a 3/4" x 8" strip of main fabric. Subcut into 1 1/4" segments and sew to top of set-up.

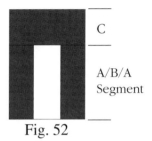

Fig. 52

ASSEMBLY

Cut (2) 1" x 44" strips of background fabric for sashing.

1.   Subcut (3) 3 1/4" lengths. Sew three rows: house block/strip/house block.

2.   Subcut (4) 7" lengths. Sew between the rows and to the top and bottom.

3.   Subcut (2) 12 1/4" strips and sew to sides. If your houses are a little shorter than 3" high, adjust these side strips accordingly.

Fig. 53

Borders

1.   Cut (4) 3/4" x 44" strips of main fabric.

2.   Cut (2) 3/4" x 44" strips of background fabric.

3.   Sew these strips into 1 1/2 set-ups (one 44" and one 22"), (Fig. 53).

4.   With the remaining one-half strip lengths, sew this set-up, (Fig. 54).

5.   Subcut first set-up into (2) 8 1/2" lengths; (2) 12 1/4" lengths; and (4) 3/4" segments.

6.   Subcut second set-up into (8) 3/4" segments. Stitch these segments into (4) Nine-Patch set-ups, (Fig. 55).

7.   Stitch a Nine-Patch to each end of the 8 1/2" lengths.

8.   Stitch the 12 1/4" lengths to the sides of the quilt.

9.   Stitch the top and bottom border to the quilt.

Fig. 54

Layer the quilt with batting and backing. Quilt and bind as desired.

Fig. 55

TWISTING STAR

quilt shown on page 33

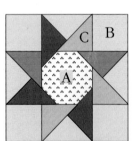

3" Finished Block

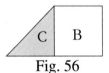

Fig. 56

Fig. 57

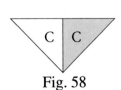

Fig. 58   Fig. 59

12" x 16"

This star looks very difficult to piece, but it can be done quite easily. Marsha McCloskey's book, Lessons in Machine Piecing, *presents this star in a 10" block size. The design is also included as a larger block in Judy Martin's* Ultimate Book of Quilt Block Patterns. *Its unique octagonal shape made me eager to try it in miniature.*

FABRIC REQUIREMENTS
Scraps for blocks
5/8 yard for background, backing and binding
1/8 yard accent for border; 5/8 yard if using a printed stripe

The instructions below are for one block so that each block can be made of different fabrics. If you desire to make all blocks the same, multiply the numbers shown in parentheses by six.

CUTTING
A. Octagon: Cut (1) 1 1/2" square of accent fabric. Cut off each corner using square ruler by aligning diagonal line of ruler on straight edge of corner and 7/16" marking on other straight edge of same corner. Cut off angle. Repeat procedure for all four corners.
B. Cut (4) 1 1/8" squares of light background fabric.
C. Triangles: (4) of light background fabric and (8) of medium to dark fabrics. The long sides must be cut on the straight grain of the fabric. Cut (1) 1 15/16" square of the light background fabric and (2) 1 15/16" squares of medium to dark fabrics. Cut each of these squares diagonally both ways.

PIECING
1. Chain-piece (4) B/C-dark units, (Fig. 56). Place C-dark triangles on top of squares when stitching. Press seams toward triangles, (Fig. 57).
2. Chain-piece (4) C-dark/C-light units, (Fig. 58). Place dark triangles on top of background triangles when stitching, (Fig. 59). Press seams toward dark triangles.
3. Arrange C/C units and B/C-dark units in place around the octagon, (Fig. 60). Take units in consecutive order as you sew them to the octagon.
4. Place the first C/C unit face down on one side of the octagon, (Fig.61). Begin stitching at the edge of the triangle and stop stitching halfway on the side of the octagon. Backtack. Press seam away from center.

5.   Sew the first C/C unit to the previous section (Fig. 62). Press away from center.
6.   Continue stitching other units alternately as above and pressing seams away from center. Push the free edge of the unit that was first sewn onto the octagon out of the way to sew on the last unit (C/B).
7.   Place free edges of C/C unit and C/B unit together and complete seam. Press.

ASSEMBLY

1.   Center Square: Cut (1) 3 1/4" square of a background fabric that contrasts with the background fabric of the stars.
2.   Setting Triangles: You will need (10) triangles with long sides on straight of grain of fabric. Cut (3) 5 1/2" squares and cut diagonally both ways. For each corner sew the short sides of two triangles together.
3.   Assemble quilt as illustrated.
4.   First Border: Cut (2) 7/8" x 44" strips of accent fabric. I used a printed striped fabric and mitered the corners.
5.   Second Border: Cut (2) 1 3/8" x 44" strips of background fabric. If you are using a printed stripe fabric for the first border, sew the first and second border strips together and then miter the corners as one unit.
6.   Layer the quilt with batting and backing. Quilt and bind as desired.

Fig. 60

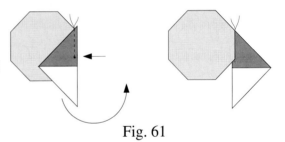

Fig. 61

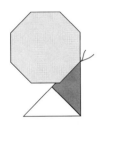 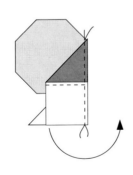 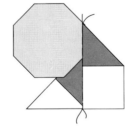

Fig. 62

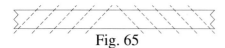

13" Square

For a long time, I could not figure out why this traditional design is called California Star when the center consists of Ohio Star blocks. My question was answered in an old book called The Romance of the Patchwork Quilt in America *which says that a feathered star with a Nine-Patch in the center is given this name. My quilt has only two colors, but you could put a third color in the big triangles of the outer star points and the plain squares of the center block. Do make sure there is good contrast between the "feathers" and background.*

FABRIC REQUIREMENTS
1/2 yard main fabric and binding
1/2 yard background and backing

CUTTING AND PIECING
Ohio Stars Center Block
1.   Make perfectly pieced quarter-square triangle units, (Fig. 63). Cut 1" wide bias strips of dark and background fabrics, totaling approximately 45" of each. Sew same size strips of dark and background fabrics together. Press seams to dark fabric. Subcut these strips into 1" segments. (Need 40.) Sew (2) 1" segments together to make a Four-Patch unit. Place the square ruler's diagonal line on the vertical seam with 7/8" line markings on the horizontal seam. Cut off the top two angles; reverse the ruler and cut a 7/8" bias square of 1/4-square triangles, (Fig. 64). (Need 20.)
2.   Cut (1) 7/8" x 20" strip of background fabric. Subcut into (20) squares.
3.   Cut (5) 7/8" squares of dark fabric.
4.   Assemble the (5) Ohio Stars as shown in picture.
5.   Assemble the entire center block.

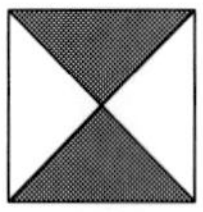

Cutting the Star Points
1.   Cut (4) 2 5/16" squares of dark fabric. Cut these squares diagonally to make (8) triangles.
2.   Cut (2) 7/8" squares of dark fabric. Cut each square diagonally to make (4) triangles.
3.   Cut 7/8" wide bias strips, totaling about 60" each of dark and background fabrics. Sew same size strips together. Press seams to dark fabric. Cut (48) 11/16" bias squares.
4.   Cut 1" wide bias strips totaling about 36" each of dark and background fabrics. Sew same size strips together. Press seams to dark fabric. Cut (24) 7/8" bias squares
5.   Cut (8) diamonds for ends of star points. First cut (1) 7/8" x 12" strip of dark fabric. At left end of strip cut a 45° angle with square ruler. Measure over 11/16" and cut another angle parallel to the 45° angle. Repeat to cut (3) more diamonds going this direction. Now move over on

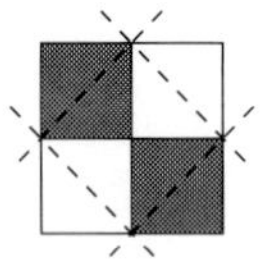

Fig. 63

Fig. 64

Fig. 65

your strip and cut a 45° angle going in the reverse direction. Cut (4) diamonds, (Fig. 65).
6.   Cut (4) 1 1/16" squares of background fabric. Cut these diagonally to make (8) triangles.
7.   Cut (4) 7/8" squares of background fabric. Cut these diagonally to make (8) triangles.

Piecing the Star Points
1.   Piece (4) Unit A's. These are the 11/16" bias squares.

2.   Piece (4) Unit B's. These are the 11/16" bias squares.

3.   Piece (4) Unit C's. These are the 7/8" bias squares. Use the diamonds which were cut to the left.

4.   Piece (4) Unit D's. These are the 7/8" bias squares. Use the diamonds which were cut to the right.

5.   Stitch Unit A's to inside of left dark triangles, (Fig. 66).
6.   Stitch Units B's to inside of right dark triangles, (Fig. 67).
7.   Stitch Unit C's to outside of left dark triangles, (Fig. 68).
8.   Stitch Unit D's to outside of right dark triangles, (Fig. 69).
9.   Cut (1) 7" square of background fabric and cut diagonally both ways to make (4) setting triangles for star points. (They are a little large in order to float the California Star.)
10.   Stitch (4) of these units together, (Fig. 70).

ASSEMBLY
1.   Cut (4) 3 3/4" squares of background fabric for the corner squares. These corner squares are a little large.
2.   Assemble all pieced units and corner squares. Trim setting triangles and corners evenly to about 1/2" from the end of the diamond points.
3.   Layer quilt with batting and backing. Quilt and bind as desired.

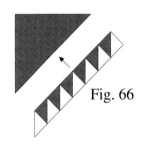

Fig. 66

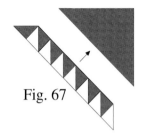

Fig. 67

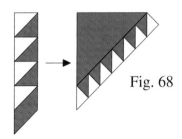

Fig. 68

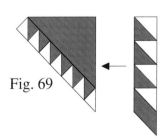

Fig. 69

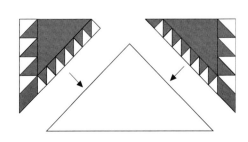

Fig. 70

SPINNING PINWHEELS  quilt shown on page 32

9 1/2" x 12 1/2"
12 Blocks

This traditional pattern dates back to a book from the 1930s. By first sewing strips together and then cutting triangles from these strips, you can put the blocks together precisely and quickly. Placing the blocks on point and using a darker fabrics for the setting triangles makes a charming border for these tiny "spinning" pinwheels.

FABRIC REQUIREMENTS
Option 1: All pinwheel blocks from same fabrics
    1/4 yard light background for A and C
    1/4 yard medium for B
    1/8 yard dark for D
Option 2: Each pinwheel block of different fabrics
    (12) 8" squares of various lights for A and C
    (12) 8" squares of various mediums for B
    (12) 1 1/2" x 8" strips of various darks for D
    1/8 yard medium light for center background blocks
    1/4 yard dark for setting triangles, corners, and binding
    3/8 yard for backing

CUTTING
Option 1—To make all (12) blocks the same, cut:
A. Background Fabric: (12) 1 3/8" x 8" bias strips. First, cut a 7" x 44" strip crossgrain on the fabric. Using the 45° angle line on the ruler, make a bias cut on the left side of this strip. Cut (12) 1 3/8" wide bias strips, measuring from each bias cut.
B. Medium Fabric: (12) 1 3/8" bias strips. Follow above cutting procedure.
C. Background Fabric: (2) 3/4" x 44" strips.
D. Dark Fabric: (2) 1 1/2" x 44" strips.

Option 2—To make each block of different fabrics, cut:
A. Background Fabrics: (12) different 1 3/8" x 8" bias strips.
B. Medium Fabrics: (12) different 1 3/8" x 8" bias strips.
C. Background Fabrics: (12) different 3/4" x 8" strips on the straight-of-grain.
D. Dark Fabrics: (12) different 1 1/2" x 8" strips on the straight-of-grain.

PIECING
1. Make (48) A/B Units, (Fig. 71): Seam A strips to B strips lengthwise. Press seams to medium fabrics. Turn A/B strips so that medium fabric is on the left. Cut a straight edge on bottom. Using the square ruler, align the diagonal line on the

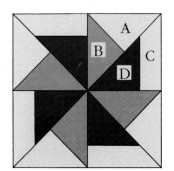

2" Finished Block

seam line and 1 7/16" markings on straight edge of bottom. Cut A/B triangle. Cut a new straight edge on the bottom and continue this cutting procedure.

2.   Make (48) C/D Units, (Fig. 72): Seam C strips to D strips lengthwise. Press seams to dark fabrics. Trim edge on light fabrics to exactly 3/8" from seam line. Next trim edge on dark fabrics to 1 7/16" from edge of light fabrics. Cut a straight edge on one end and cut 1 7/16" squares. Now cut across each square on the diagonal so that the dark fabric is the upper portion.

3.   Stitch A/B units to C/D units. Press seams toward C/D units.

4.   Stitch the new combination into pairs. It is helpful to first cut the points off the ends. Press seams toward dark fabric.

5.   Now stitch two sets of pairs together for each block.

ASSEMBLY

1.   Cut (6) 2 1/4" squares of light background fabric.

2.   Cut (3) 4 1/8" squares of background fabric (can be the same as the six background blocks or a darker shade) and cut both ways diagonally. You need (10) setting triangles, (Fig. 73).

3.   Cut (2) 3" squares and cut diagonally to make (4) corner triangles.

4.   Assemble as shown. Using the square ruler, trim the four corners even with the side of the quilt.

5.   Layer the quilt with batting and backing. Quilt and bind as desired.

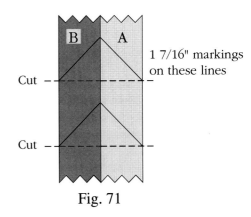

Fig. 71

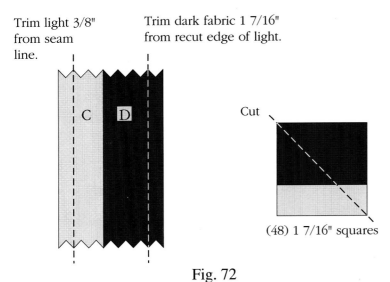

Fig. 72

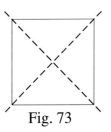

Fig. 73

LEXINGTON STRIPPY QUILT

quilt shown on page 32

13 3/4" x 19"

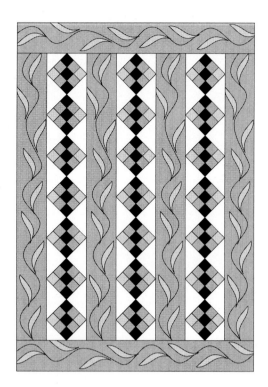

While on vacation I purchased the printed striped fabric in Lexington, Kentucky. I was inspired by a reference to "The Spectacular Strippy" quilts made in the late 1700s to mid 1800s in the book Threads of Time *by Nancy J. Martin. This fabric was "made" for a miniature strippy quilt.*

FABRIC REQUIREMENTS
Scraps for blocks
3/4 yard for background and backing
3/4 yard printed stripe for border strips and binding

CUTTING—for (21) blocks
1.   Cut (63) 3/4" squares from one dark fabric. Cut a 3/4" x 44" strip, plus a 3/4" x 9" long strip. Subcut strips into 3/4" squares.
2.   Cut (126) 3/4" squares of light or medium fabrics of various coordinating colors.

PIECING—for (21) blocks
1.   Chain-piece (42) pairs of the light and medium squares together. Mix up the squares in any combination.

2.   Chain-piece a dark square to one end of each of the (42) pairs. Press seams away from center.

3.   Chain-piece a dark square to (21) single squares.

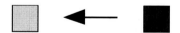

4.   Chain-piece a light or medium square to the end of the dark squares in the last set-up. Press seams toward center.

5.   Chain piece the above into (21) Nine-Patch blocks.

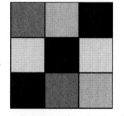

1 1/2" Finished Block

CUTTING AND PIECING OTHER UNITS

1. Cut (2) 1 3/4" x 44" strips of background fabric. Subcut into (54) 1 3/4" squares.
2. Piece (3) set-ups of Nine-Patch strips, (Fig. 74). Trim the sides of the strips back evenly, leaving a 1/8" seam allowance.
3. From the border fabric, cut (4) 2 1/8" x 15 1/8" strips. These strips will alternate with the Nine-Patch strips. The width of these strips can vary depending on the printed stripe.
4. Cut (1) 2 1/2" wide strip of border fabric for the top and bottom borders of the quilt.

ASSEMBLY

1. Stitch the (4) border strips and (3) Nine-Patch strips together alternately.
2. Measure width across quilt. Cut top and bottom borders from the 2 1/2" wide strip to fit the quilt. The width of your quilt will be determined by the width of the printed stripe used between the Nine-Patch strips.
3. Layer the quilt with batting and backing. Quilt and bind as desired.

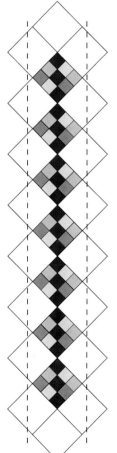

Fig. 74

SOUTHERN MAMMY QUILT quilt shown on page 37

10 1/2" x 13 1/2"

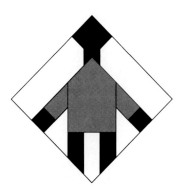

2 1/2" Finished Block

Fig.75

Fig.76

Variations of this pattern have been handed down from the slaves of the Civil War days. Rather than use many templates to cut the different shapes, set-ups can be sewn together and then cut to the exact size with the square ruler.

FABRIC REQUIREMENTS
Scraps for blocks
1/2 yard medium light background and backing
1/2 yard first border if using printed stripe; 1/8 yard if using crosswise stripe
1/4 yard dark second border and binding

CUTTING AND PIECING
Dress Segment
1.   Cut a 2 3/4" square of each dress fabric.
2.   Cut a 1 7/16" x 1 15/16" rectangle from each of these squares. Keep the remaining portion.
3.   Center the diagonal line of the square ruler on the length of each rectangle, with the corner of the two angles at the top edge of the rectangle. Cut off the two angles, (Fig. 75).

Leg Segments
1.   Cut an 11/16"x 16" bias strip of black fabric. Divide this strip in half. Cut an 11/16" x 8" bias strip of background fabric.
2.   Sew the three strips together. Press seams to black fabric.
3.   Subcut into (6) 1 1/4" segments.
4.   Center the diagonal line of the square ruler on the background strip of each segment, with the corner of the two angles at the top edge. Cut off the two angles, (Fig. 76).

Arm Segment (Right and Left)
1.   Cut a 5/8" x 13" strip of black fabric and subcut into (12) 1" pieces.
2.   Cut a 5/8" x 2 1/2" strip from the remaining portion of each of the dress fabric squares. Divide these into (2) 5/8" x 1 1/4" pieces.
3.   Cut a 1 1/4" x 27" strip of background fabric. Divide in half.
4.   Chain-piece (12) pairs of black and dress fabric pieces end-to-end. Press seams to dress fabric, (Fig. 77).
5.   Take one of the background strips and chain-piece (6) dress/hand units to the left side of the strip (hand down). Take the other background strip and chain-piece (6) dress/hand units to the right side of the strip (hand down). Press seams toward the arms.

6.	Cut each of these units straight across, 1/2" below each sleeve seam. Place diagonal line of square ruler on the edge of the sleeve/hand edge and line up the 1" intersecting lines on the diagonal line with the bottom cut edge. Cut a 45° angle, (Fig. 78).

Head
Cut (6) 7/8" squares of black fabric.

Neck and Background Segments
1.	Cut a 7/8" x 27" strip of background fabric. Subcut into (12) 2 1/8" pieces.
2.	Cut a 1/2" x 7" strip of black fabric. Subcut into (12) 1/2" squares.
3.	Stitch connector squares onto the background strips to make the neck, (Fig. 79). Press squares to corners. Trim seams to 1/8".

BLOCK ASSEMBLY
1.	Chain-piece dress segments to leg segments. Press seams toward dress fabric.
2.	Stitch arm triangles to each side of the above units. Press seams toward corners.
3.	Stitch the head squares to the right neck/background units. Press seams toward the neck.
4.	Stitch left neck/background units to the left side of body squares. Press seams toward body.
5.	Stitch last seam, and press toward neck/background.

QUILT ASSEMBLY
1.	Cut (2) 2 3/4" squares of medium light background fabric for center squares.
2.	From same fabric, cut (2) 5" squares and cut both ways diagonally for setting triangles. You will need (6) triangles.
3.	From same fabric, cut (2) 3 1/2" squares, and cut in half diagonally for corners.
4.	Assemble quilt as in picture.
5.	First Border: Cut (1) 3/4" x 44" strip of accent or printed stripe fabric and stitch to quilt using straight-cut corner method.
6.	Second Border: Cut (2) 1 1/2" x 44" strips and stitch to quilt using straight-cut corner method.
7.	Layer quilt with batting and backing. Quilt and bind as desired.

Fig. 77

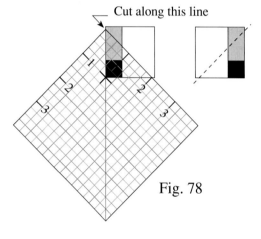

Cut along this line

Fig. 78

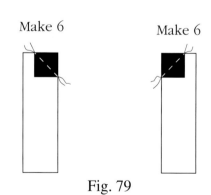

Make 6   Make 6

Fig. 79

59

DELECTABLE MOUNTAIN LAKES — quilt shown on page 37 —

Approximately 14" square
12 Blocks

    Pilgrim's Progress, *written in 1675, inspired this design. I chose a hand-dyed blue fabric to represent the cool beauty and serenity of mountain lakes in this traditional pattern. "He that formeth the mountains...the Lord, the God of hosts, is his name." Amos 4:13.*

FABRIC REQUIREMENTS
1/4 yard purple and green print for mountain base
Scraps in various purples for peaks
1/4 yard light, cool blue for lakes. (Some hand-dyed fabrics have a mottled look which resembles lakes.)
5/8 yard white for background and backing
1/4 yard for border and binding

CUTTING AND PIECING
1.   For (100) 3/4" bias squares of various purples combined with background fabric: Cut a 6" x 44" strip of white. Subcut into (17) 7/8" wide bias strips. Cut (17) 7/8" wide bias strips of various purple fabrics. It is best to have good contrast in these bias squares. Seam a white strip lengthwise to each purple strip. Cut the (100) 3/4" bias squares from these combinations.
2.   (12) 2 1/4" bias squares of the mountain base fabric and lake fabric combination: Cut an 8" x 18" rectangle of each fabric and place them right sides together. Cut (4) 2" wide bias strips on this double layer. Sew each pair together lengthwise. Press seams toward dark fabric. Cut (12) 2 1/4" bias squares.
3.   Cut (8) 3/4" squares of background and assemble blocks.

ASSEMBLY
1.   Setting Triangles: You need (4) triangles with the straight of the grain on the long side. Cut (1) 4 1/4" square of background fabric and cut diagonally both ways. These are a little large; they will be trimmed later.
2.   Corner Triangles: Cut (2) 4" squares of background fabric and cut in half diagonally.
3.   Assemble the quilt. Trim setting triangles and corner triangles evenly around the quilt, leaving a seam allowance.
4.   Borders: Cut (2) 2 1/4" x 44" strips of border fabric. Subcut to fit and stitch to quilt using straight-cut corner method.
5.   Layer the quilt with batting and backing. Quilt and bind as desired.

4 Blocks   8 Blocks
2 1/2" Finished Blocks

quilt shown on page 31

CHALLENGE OF THE UNKNOWN STARS

7" x 9"

This "very miniature" quilt made up of 1 1/2" Unknown Stars and 1/4" squares in Four-Patch units could certainly prove to be a challenge to piece. However, by sewing larger units and cutting them to a smaller size simplifies it a great deal. The method I devised to make these long, skinny triangles can be adapted for any size Unknown Star.

FABRIC REQUIREMENTS
3/8 yard for main fabric and binding
3/8 yard for background and backing

Unit A. (Need 24.)

Unit B. (Need 18.)

Unit C. (Need 34)

Unit D. (Need 48.)

Unit E. (Need 30.)

Unit F. (Need 4.)

CUTTING AND PIECING
Unit A—In order to cut the correct 64° angle for making triangles that are twice as long as they are wide, you must mark a 64° angle on a medium size ruler. (I use a 6" x 12" ruler.) On paper, draw a rectangle that is twice as long as it is wide. Draw lines connecting two opposite corners.

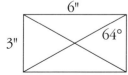

Cut out the rectangle. Tape it face down on the top of your ruler so that the long edge is aligned with a straight cross section on the ruler. Turn the ruler over. Now very carefully

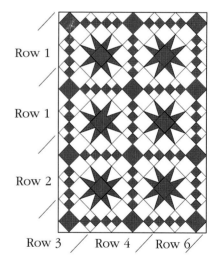

Row 1

Row 1

Row 2

Row 3   Row 4   Row 6

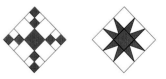

1 1/2" Finished Blocks

61

Fig. 80

2"

6"

Fig. 81

Fig. 82

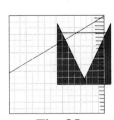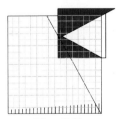

Fig. 83

Fig. 84

Fig. 85a   Fig. 85b

place drafting tape or 1/4" wide quilter's tape beneath each of the lines. Remove the paper rectangle from the top of the ruler, (Fig. 80).

1.   Cut a 1 1/2" x 44" strip of background fabric.
2.   Using the 64° angle markings on the ruler, cut (24) 64° angle triangles.

Lay the 64° angle lines of ruler on straight edges of fabric strip. You can use alternate lines without turning the ruler over or upside down.
3.   Cut a 2" x 44" strip of main fabric. Leave the strip folded in half. Subcut this strip into (12) 1" segments making 24 rectangles, (Fig. 81). Cut each of these segments diagonally in half, (Fig. 82). Each of these double segments will provide a left and right triangle for two units.
4.   Sew a left and right triangle to each center triangle. It is easiest to sew with the center triangle on top. Leave a 1/4" seam allowance at the top even though you are stitching the sides with a 1/8" seam allowance. Press seams to sides of unit, (Fig. 83).
5.   With the square ruler, trim the top section of each unit to an exact 1/8" seam allowance. Be careful to keep base of center triangle parallel to a straight line on ruler, (Fig. 84). Now turn unit upside down and place the 3/8" line of the square ruler on the center of the unit. Cut off the right edge, (Fig. 85a).

FORMULA: Use line on square ruler that is 1/2 of required cut size. Here 3/8" is 1/2 of the 3/4" required cut size. In order to adapt this method to various size units, cut the center triangles strip about 1" wider than the final cut size of unit required. Cut strip for side triangles about 1/2" wider than first strip.

Cut 3/4" square unit by lining up square ruler on the first two cut edges and cut other two sides, (Fig. 85b).

Unit B—Cut a 3/4" x 15" strip of main fabric and subcut into (18) 3/4" squares.

Unit C—Cut (1 1/2) 3/4" wide strips of background fabric and main fabric. Sew (1 1/2) sets of a background fabric strip and main fabric strip together. Subcut into (68) 3/4" segments. Chain-piece (34) Four-Patch units, (Fig. 86). Align 3/8" square of ruler on upper right square of Four-Patch. Cut two sides. Align 3/4" square with the two cut edges and cut other two sides of Four-Patch unit, (Fig. 87).

Unit D—Cut a 3/4" x 44" strip of background fabric. Subcut into (48) 3/4" squares.

Unit E—Cut (8) 3 1/4" squares of background fabric and cut both ways diagonally for setting triangles. (Need 30.)

Unit F—Cut (2) 2 1/2" squares of background fabric and cut in half diagonally for corner triangles. (Need 4.)

ASSEMBLY
1.   Make (6) Unknown Star blocks. Press seams of Units A (points) toward B or D (squares).
2.   Make (2) complete Single Irish Chain blocks.
3.   Various partial Single Irish Chain blocks are necessary to complete the quilt top. Make (4) partial Single Irish Chain blocks, (Fig. 88). The small Unit E setting triangles are too large on purpose. Place the bias edges on the bottom of the squares when stitching. After the entire large setting triangle unit is completed, trim the edges evenly, leaving a 1/8" seam allowance.
4.   Make (2) partial Single Irish Chain blocks to be used as setting triangles for the top and bottom of the quilt, (Fig. 89). Trim the edges evenly, leaving a 1/8" seam allowance.
5.   Make (2) partial Single Irish Chain blocks to be used for the upper right corner and for the lower left corner of the quilt, (Fig. 90). Trim the edges evenly, leaving a 1/8" seam allowance.
6.   Make (2) partial Single Irish Chain blocks as illustrated, to be used for the upper left corner and for the lower right corner of the quilt, (Fig. 91). Trim the edges evenly, leaving a 1/8" seam allowance.
7.   Assemble complete and partial blocks into rows.
8.   Border: Cut (1) 1 1/4" x 44" strip of background fabric. Subcut to fit. Stitch borders to sides of quilt first and then to the top and bottom using straight-cut corner method.
9.   Layer the quilt with batting and backing. Quilt and bind as desired.

Fig. 86

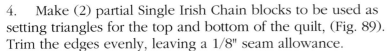

Fig. 87

Fig. 88

Fig. 89

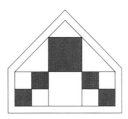

Fig. 90

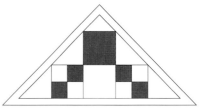

Fig. 91

STAR LIGHT, STAR BRIGHT quilt shown on page 31

14 1/2" x 14 1/2"

This quilt is made up of alternating Unknown Stars and Snowball blocks. I designed it for a block challenge at our local quilt shop. Omitting parts of the pattern from the outer blocks and adding a border strip of background fabric creates a galaxy of floating Unknown Stars.

FABRIC REQUIREMENTS
1/2 yard light for background and backing
Assorted blue scraps for star points and Snowball corners
Assorted black or gray scraps for squares of Unknown Star blocks
1/4 yard for border and binding

CUTTING AND PIECING
Snowball Blocks
1.   Cut (1) 2 1/2" x 44" strip of background fabric. Subcut (13) 2 1/2" squares. (Option: Cut from assorted background fabrics.)
2.   Cut (32) 1" squares from assorted blue fabrics.
3.   Make (13) Snowball Blocks using connector corner method (page 13), (Fig. 92). Press each square to its corner and trim seam.

Unknown Star Blocks
1.   Make (48) star point units, (Fig. 93). These triangles are cut at a 64° angle, which must be marked on your ruler. (I use a 6" x 12" ruler.) On paper, draw a rectangle that is twice as long as it is wide. Draw connecting lines to opposite corners, (Fig. 94). Cut out the rectangle. Tape it face down on the top of your ruler. Turn the ruler over and place drafting tape or 1/4" quilter's tape beneath each of the lines on the bottom of the ruler, (Fig. 95). Remove the paper.
2.   Cut (2) 2" x 44" strips of background fabric.
3.   Using the 64° angle on the ruler, cut (48) center triangles, (Fig. 96). Lay the 64° angle on either straight edge of the strip. You can use alternate lines without turning the ruler over or upside down.
4.   Cut (12) 2 1/2" x 5" rectangles of assorted blue fabrics for star points. Subcut each of these rectangles into (4) 1 1/4" x 2 1/2" rectangles. Place (2) rectangles wrong sides together and cut in half diagonally. Repeat for other rectangles, (Fig. 97). Each 2 1/2" x 5" rectangle provides all the star points for one star.
5.   Sew a left and right triangle to each center triangle, (Fig. 98). Leave 1/4" seam allowance at the top, even though you are using 1/8" seams. Press seams to sides of units.

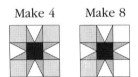

Make 4   Make 8

2 1/4" Finished Blocks

2 1/4" Finished Blocks

Make 4   Make 4   Make 5

Fig. 92

Fig. 93

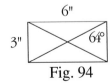

Fig. 94

6.   Using the square ruler, trim the top section of each unit to an exact 1/8" seam allowance. Keep the base of the center triangle parallel to a straight line on the ruler, (Fig. 99). Turn unit and place 1/2" line on ruler on the center of the unit. Cut off the right edge, (Fig. 100).

FORMULA: Use line on square ruler that is one-half the cut size needed. Here 1/2" is one-half of the 1" cut size unit needed.

Cut 1" square unit by lining up the 1" lines of the square ruler on the two cut edges and cut the other two sides, (Fig. 101).
7.   Cut (44) 1" squares from assorted black or gray scraps. I used one fabric for the (12) center squares.
8.   Cut (16) 1" squares from background fabric.
9.   Assemble star blocks as illustrated: (4) stars with (4) dark corners; (8) stars with (2) background corners and (2) dark corners. Press seams of star point units toward squares.

ASSEMBLY
1.   Arrange blocks and sew them together.
2.   First Border: Cut (2) 3/4" x 44" strips of background fabric. Subcut to fit and stitch to quilt using straight-cut corner method. This border acts as a floater strip.
3.   Second Border: Cut (2) 1 1/2" x 44" strips of dark fabric. Subcut to fit and sew to quilt using straight-cut corner method.
4.   Layer quilt with batting and backing. Quilt and bind as desired.

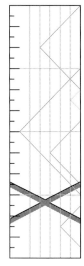

Fig. 95

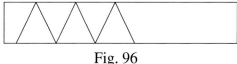

Fig. 96

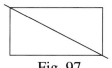

Fig. 97

Fig. 98

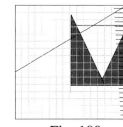

Fig. 99

Fig. 100

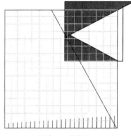

Fig. 101

BIBLIOGRAPHY

Gravatt, Tina M., *Heirloom Miniatures*, American Quilter's Society, Paduch, KY, 1990.

Hall, Carrie A., and Rose G. Krᵉtsinger, *The Romance of the Patchwork Quilt in America*, Bonanza Books, Crown Publishers, Inc., New York, 1935.

Hargrave, Harriet, *Heirloom Machine Quilting*, C&T Publishing, Lafayette, CA, 1990.

Hickey, Mary, *Little By Little: Quilts in Miniature*, That Patchwork Place, Inc., Bothell, Washington, 1988.

Hopkins, Mary Ellen, *The It's Okay If You Sit On My Quilt Book*, Burdette Publications, Westminster, CA, 1982.

————, *Connecting Up*, ME Publications, Santa Monica, CA 90404, 1990.

Hughes, Trudie, *More Template-Free Quiltmaking*, That Patchwork Place, Inc., Bothell, WA, 1987

————, *Template-Free Quilts and Borders*, That Patchwork Place, Inc., Bothell, WA, 1990.

Martin, Nancy J., *Pieces of the Past*, That Patchwork Place Inc., Bothell, WA, Second Edition, 1986.

————, *Threads of Time*, That Patchwork Place, Inc., Bothell, WA 1990.

McCloskey, Marsha, *Lessons in Machine Piecing*, That Patchwork Place, Bothell, WA, 1990.

————, *Feathered Star Quilts*, That Patchwork Place, Bothell, WA, 1987.

"Miniature Quilts Magazine," Chitra Publications, Montrose, PA. 1989—.

Schaefer, Becky, *Working In Miniature*, C&T Publishing, Lafayette, CA, 1987.

Srebro, Nancy Johnson, *Miniature to Masterpiece*, RCW Publishing Co., Columbia Crossroads, PA, 1990.

Thomas, Donna Lynn, *Small Talk*, That Patchwork Place, Bothell, WA, 1991.